Countdown to French GCSE

A ten-day revision workbook to prepare you for the exam

About the author

Lucy Martin was educated in Brussels and the UK and has a first-class degree in Modern Languages from Wadham College, Oxford. She speaks five languages and teaches to all levels, with a superb track record in top exam results. She is a contributor to BBC Bitesize and has written twelve books for students of French, Spanish and German. She lives in London with her three children.

Copyright Lucy Martin 2019

www.lucymartintuition.co.uk

Table of contents

Introduction   5

Day 1 – Gender, adjectives, infinitives, describing people   7

Day 2 – Present tense, describing places and town / home   25

Day 3 – Direct and indirect pronouns, health and hobbies   49

Day 4 – Past tense, the food topic and past activities   65

Day 5 – Imperfect tense, your childhood and holidays   83

Day 6 – Future tense, education and jobs   93

Day 7 – Conditional, ideals, technology   105

Day 8 – Subjunctive and social / environment topics   115

Day 9 – Special constructions, negatives, pros and cons   129

Day 10 – Listening tips, the writing mnemonic, exam tips   141

This book is dedicated to every single one of you who is taking GCSE or IGCSE French this year. Good luck!

Introduction

I produced this book in response to demand from students and parents looking for a day by day revision and study guide. There are plenty of grammar and vocabulary books on the market, but there was a call for something that could be studied in bitesize chunks and was not too overwhelming in terms of content.

The ten chapters take you through all the essentials of the GCSE syllabus in terms of grammar, vocabulary and oral answers, with a special section at the end on tips and strategies for the listening and writing papers. So rather than spend a whole day learning vocabulary, you focus on a few grammar points followed by exercises on those points, then a short vocabulary list and oral questions and answers that relate to the grammar and vocabulary of the day.

I have limited it to ten chapters so that it is a manageable task for the Christmas holidays (before the mock exams) or the Easter holidays (before the main exams). There is a fair bit of material in each chapter, so depending on your current level, you may take a couple of hours to complete the work in each. Ideally, you should complete the book once at Christmas and then again at Easter, by which time it should be a much faster process.

Don't forget that you can also watch the videos on my Lucy Martin Tuition YouTube channel which will help you get through the oral and the writing by focusing on standard impressive answers that you can adapt to suit individual questions. These standard answers are in this book in text boxes.

Finally, I am always keen to hear from my readers and fellow teachers and tutors. Please don't hesitate to get in touch via my website www.lucymartintuition.co.uk

NOTES

Day 1

In this session you will be revising:

- Nouns and their articles
- Adjectives and their agreements
- Infinitives and when to use them
- Vocabulary on family and general topics
- How to describe your family and a family member or friend

Nouns and Gender

Nouns in French are masculine or feminine.

The indefinite article un, une

The word for "a" or "an" is either **un or une** depending on whether the noun is masculine (un chien – a dog) or feminine (une table – a table). There are a few rules to help you work out the gender of nouns but generally you need to learn each word with its gender.

The definite article le, la, les

The definite article "the" is **le, la or les** but special rules apply to it.

- Use it when we say **the** in English:

Le for masculine nouns	le chien = the dog
La for feminine nouns	la maison = the house
Les for plural nouns	les enfants = the children

- Use it for **generalisations**:

Les chiens sont sympas	Dogs are nice
Le chocolat est délicieux	Chocolate is delicious

- Use it with **school subjects**:

J'étudie l'histoire	I am studying history

- Use it when talking about **liking, hating, disliking, preferring**

J'aime **les** chiens	I like dogs
Je préfère **les** chats	I prefer cats
J'aime **la** pizza	I like pizza
J'adore **la** neige	I love snow
Je déteste **la** viande	I hate meat
Je n'aime pas **les** documentaires	I don't like documentaries

Adjectives

- **Adjectives go after the noun,** except in a few cases which include: *grand, petit, joli, nouveau, vieux, bon, beau, mauvais, gros.*

- **They agree** with the noun they are describing : "Il est grand" but "elle est grand**e**" and "elles sont grand**es**" etc. Adjectives like *petit, grand, amusant, bavard, marrant, intelligent* take an e for the feminine and an s for plural. Others are more complicated. For a list of adjectives and their feminine forms, look at the vocabulary lists overleaf.

- **They don't agree after c'est** (it is). After c'est or c'était, the adjective is always masculine.

- **Some don't agree at all!** (see list) usually because they end in an "e" or because the adjective is an abbreviation (sympa), or a compound word (casse-pieds).

- Use the **comparative** or **superlative** to improve your mark:

plus…………que	more …………… than
moins……….que	less ……………... than
le meilleur collège de Londres	the best school in London
la meilleure ville du monde	the best town in the world

- You can **qualify** your adjective using:

très	very
assez	quite
extrêmement	extremely
parfois	sometimes
toujours	always
un peu	a bit

Common adjectives with their feminine forms – test yourself!

grand(e) / petit(e)	tall / small
gros(se)	fat
bavard(e)	chatty
marrant(e)	funny
intéressant(e)	interesting
embêtant(e)	annoying
joli(e)	pretty
fort(e)	strong
fâché(e)	angry
méchant(e)	naughty
gentil(-le)	kind
ennuyeux/-euse	boring
paresseux/-euse	lazy
sérieux/-euse	serious
heureux/-euse	happy
sportif/-ive	sporty
vieux (vieille)	old
beau (belle)	beautiful
mince	thin
sympa	nice
égoïste	selfish
jeune	young
moche	ugly
agréable	pleasant

"My" and other possessive adjectives

Whereas in English, you say *my* regardless of the noun that follows, in French, the word for *my* varies according to the gender and number of the thing that you own.

mon with masculine nouns	mon chien = my dog
ma with feminine nouns	ma maison = my house
mes with plural nouns	mes parents = my parents

Your (**ton, ta, tes**) and *his* or *her* (**son, sa, ses**) follow the same rule. Remember that there is no separate word for "his" and "her", Both are son/sa/ses, so you will need to determine meaning from the context.

son père	his/her father
sa mère	his/her mother
ses parents	his/her parents
tes amis	your friends
ta sœur	your sister
ton frère	your brother

In the plural forms (our, your and their) there are only two forms – one for singular nouns and one for plural nouns.

notre père	our father
notre mère	our mother
nos parents	our parents
votre frère	your brother
votre sœur	your sister
vos amis	your friends
leur oncle	their uncle
leur tante	their aunt
leurs grands-parents	their grandparents

If you are using the pronoun *on* (meaning one, you or we), the corresponding possessive adjective is *son / sa / ses*:

Il y a un club où on peut retrouver ses amis.
There is a club where you/one can meet up with your/one's friends.

Translate

1. I like dogs

2. I don't like documentaries

3. Cats are nice

4. Bread is delicious

5. I hate chips

6. I prefer pizza

7. Your(s) friends are fun

8. His parents are quite thin

9. My house is very beautiful

10. Her brother is lazy

11. Her friends are chatty

12. Their dog is a bit naughty

13. Our friend is annoying sometimes

14. His sister is funnier than his brother

15. My grandparents are sporty

Answers

1. J'aime les chiens
2. Je n'aime pas les documentaires
3. Les chats sont sympas
4. Le pain est délicieux
5. Je déteste les frites
6. Je préfère la pizza
7. Tes amis sont amusants
8. Ses parents sont assez minces
9. Ma maison est très belle
10. Son frère est paresseux
11. Ses amis sont bavards
12. Leur chien est un peu méchant
13. Notre ami est parfois embêtant
14. Sa sœur est plus marrante que son frère
15. Mes grands-parents sont sportifs

Infinitives

These are verbs in their original form before they are conjugated. You need them for the future tense (after present tense of *aller*) and also after verbs like *j'aime, je préfère, on peut, on doit, je veux, je voudrais* and *pour*. Test yourself on these:

Aider	to help
Ranger	to tidy
Laver	to wash
Recycler	to recycle
Faire	to do
Aller	to go
Terminer	to finish
Commencer	to begin
Perdre	to lose
Chercher	to look for
Oublier	to forget
Trouver	to find
Rencontrer	to meet
Retrouver	to meet up with
Prendre	to take / have (with meals)
Apprendre	to learn
Comprendre	to understand
Venir	to come
Devenir	to become
Revenir	to come back
Sortir	to go out
Partir	to leave
Construire	to build

Conduire	to drive
Lire	to read
Dire	to say
Produire	to produce
Réduire	to reduce
Mettre	to put (or lay)
Écrire	to write
Vendre	to sell
Entendre	to hear
Travailler	to work
Monter	to go up
Montrer	to show
Fermer	to close
Ouvrir	to open
Arrêter	to stop
Dépenser	to spend
Economiser	to save
Marcher	to walk
Courir	to run
Rester	to stay
Devoir	to have to
Recevoir	to receive
Rire	to laugh
Sourire	to smile
Conseiller	to advise
Répondre	to answer
Penser	to think

Exercise using infinitives – test yourself

I like working	j'aime travailler
I prefer travelling	je préfère voyager
I don't like running	je n'aime pas courir
I'm going to forget	je vais oublier
I'm not going to lose	je ne vais pas perdre
He likes saving his money	il aime économiser son argent
We like spending	nous aimons dépenser
They don't like reading	ils n'aiment pas lire
I'd like to help	je voudrais aider
I want to be rich	je veux être riche
I want to leave	je veux partir
One can go out	on peut sortir
One can't wash the car	on ne peut pas laver la voiture
One has to recycle	on doit recycler
I don't have to come	je ne dois pas venir
I don't have to stop	je ne dois pas arrêter
I don't want to laugh	je ne veux pas rire
I'm not going to come back	je ne vais pas revenir
I have to stay	je dois rester
I have to think	je dois penser
I like laughing	j'aime rire
I don't like laying the table	je n'aime pas mettre la table
I prefer doing sport	je préfère faire du sport
I hate advising	je déteste conseiller
I'm going to stop	je vais arrêter

Vocabulary

Family

dans ma famille	in my family
nous sommes quatre	there are 4 of us
mon père	my father
ma mère	my mother
mes parents	my parents
ainé / cadet	older / younger (m)
ainée / cadette	older / younger (f)
mes grands-parents	my grandparents
mon cousin / ma cousine	my cousin
mon oncle	my uncle
ma tante	my aunt
Je suis enfant unique	I'm an only child
mon demi-frère	my half or step-brother
ma demi-sœur	my half or step-sister
mon beau-père	my father-in-law or step
ma belle-mère	my mother-in-law or step
le bébé	baby
le garçon	boy
la fille	girl or daughter
le fils	son
Mon frère s'appelle	my brother is called
Je n'ai **pas de** sœur	I don't have a sister
on s'entend bien	we get on well
beaucoup en commun	lots in common
les mêmes choses	the same things
on se dispute	we argue

Types of relationship and family

toutes sortes de familles	all sorts of families
de bons rapports	good relations
une relation	a relationship
petit copain	boyfriend
petite copine	girlfriend
un rendez-vous	a date
tomber amoureux	to fall in love
l'amour	love
rencontrer	to meet
un couple	a couple
fidèle	faithful
ensemble	together (musical)
cohabiter	to live together
avant de se marier	before getting married
se marier avec	to marry
épouser	to marry
se séparer	to separate
divorcer	to get divorced
divorcé	divorced
marié	married
séparé	separated
une famille nombreuse	a big family
une famille recomposée	a blended family
une famille monoparentale	a single parent family
le mariage gay	gay marriage
se disputer	to argue
la valeur	value

la stabilité	stability
élever un enfant	to bring up a child
adopter	to adopt

Hair adjectives

longs / courts	long / short
raides	straight
frisés / bouclés	curly
blonds / roux / marron	blonde / red / brown
Il a les cheveux marron *(no s!)*	he has brown hair
Il est chauve	he is bald

General appearance

Il porte des lunettes	he wears glasses
une barbe	beard
une moustache	moustache
Je ressemble à	I look like
On se ressemble	we look similar

Clothes

je porte	I wear
je mets	I put on
des vêtements	clothes
on doit porter	we have to wear
un uniforme	uniform

Top tip: Think about a man wearing the masculine clothes and a woman wearing the feminine clothes. It's a bit unfair, because she gets a lot more than he does, even the shirt, tie, jacket, socks and shoes. He gets jeans, trousers, a Tshirt, a jumper, coat, hat and gloves.

Masculine clothes

un pull	jumper *(pullover)*
un t-shirt	Tshirt
un jean	jeans
un pantalon	trousers *(pants long)*
un manteau	coat *(man, down to his toes)*
un chapeau	hat *(for a chap)*
un imperméable	raincoat

Feminine clothes

une veste	jacket *(not vest!)*
une robe	dress
une jupe	skirt
une chemise	shirt
une cravate	tie
une casquette	cap
une écharpe	scarf

Plural clothes

des chaussettes (f)	socks *(you need a set)*
des chaussures (f)	shoes *(be sure of them)*
des bottes (f)	boots

des baskets (f)	trainers
des gants (m)	gloves

Materials

en coton	cotton
en laine	wool
en soie	silk
en cuir	leather

Accessories

des écouteurs	earphones *(from écouter)*
des bijoux	jewellery
des lunettes	glasses
du maquillage	make-up
un portable	mobile
un parapluie	umbrella
des boucles d'oreille	earrings
un collier	necklace *(collar)*
un porte-monnaie	purse
un portefeuille	wallet *(a portfolio of money)*

Animals

un chien	a dog
un chat	a cat
un lapin	a rabbit
une vache	a cow
un cheval	a horse
un mouton	a sheep

un cochon	a pig
un cochon d'inde	a guinea pig
un poisson	a fish
J'ai un chien **qui** s'appelle	I have a dog called
Je n'ai pas **de** chien	I don't have a dog
Je n'ai pas **d'**animaux	I don't have a pet
Je voudrais **un** chien	I would like a dog

How much can you remember?
1. Name 5 masculine clothes
2. Name 5 feminine clothes
3. What's the rule about liking?
4. What are the three words for *my* and when do you use them?
5. What are the three words for *the* and when do you use them?

For your oral and writing
The standard story on family and friends

Use this story to describe any member of your family or any friend or teacher. Don't bother thinking up new hair colours and eye colours – just use the same ones each time.

Key to remembering it

Begin with the name. Remember that *s'appelle* means *is called* and *qui s'appelle* means *who is called*.

Now do three things that take avoir (age, hair and eyes)

Now three that take être (they are very … but a bit ….. and more sporty than me)

Finally, learn my long "normalement" sentence. You won't regret it!

Describing a person (take any chance you get to do this – even if you're describing an outing – say who you're going with and describe him or her)

Dans ma famille nous sommes quatre – mon père, ma mère, ma sœur et moi. Ma soeur s'appelle Daisy et elle a 15 ans. Elle a les yeux bleus et les cheveux blonds. Elle est très intelligente mais un peu timide et elle est plus sportive que moi. Normalement on s'entend bien parce que nous avons beaucoup de choses en commun comme le tennis mais quelquefois on se dispute car elle n'aime pas ma musique.

In my family there are 4 of us – my father, my mother, my sister and me. My sister is called Daisy and she is 15. She has blue eyes and blonde hair. She is very intelligent but a bit shy and she is more sporty than me. Normally we get on well because we have lots of things in common like tennis but sometimes we argue because she doesn't like my music.

Role models Un modèle à suivre devrait donner un bon exemple en tout. Il devrait être gentil, compréhensif, intelligent, et ne devrait pas être parfait. Il faut que les jeunes apprennent à se respecter sans se comparer aux autres, et il faut suivre des modèles qui montrent qu'il y a des choses plus importantes dans la vie.

A role model should give a good example in everything. They should be kind, understanding, intelligent and should not be perfect. Young people need to learn to respect themselves without comparing themselves to others, and one should have role models who show that there are more important things in life.

Day 2

In this session you will be revising:
- Verbs in the present tense
- Vocabulary relating to your town, house and routine
- How to describe your town, house and routine

Present tense

The most important verbs in French: être and avoir

These verbs don't just mean *to be* and *to have*, they are used to form the past tense – or passé composé, so you need to be very familiar with them. To revise them, recite them in a rhythm. Notice how all the *avoir* ones begin with *a* (except *ont*, but the o is almost an a…) and notice how the *sont* and the *ont* rhyme when you recite it. Picture, recite and repeat the two verbs in the order they are below.

être – to be	
Je suis	I am
Tu es	you (singular) are
Il est / elle est	he / she is
Nous sommes	we are
Vous êtes	you (plural) are
Ils sont / elles sont	they are
avoir – to have	
J'ai	I have
Tu as	you (singular) have
Il / elle a	he / she has
Nous avons	we have
Vous avez	you (plural) have
Ils ont / elles ont	they have

To make them negative, just put **ne……pas** around the verb. But with avoir, if you don't have something, use **de**.

Je ne suis pas sûr	I am not sure
Il n'est pas marrant	He's not funny
Elles ne sont pas là	They aren't there
Tu n'as pas **de** sœur ?	Don't you have a sister?

Present tense

There are three main types of regular verb in French, ending in *–er*, *-re* and *–ir*. The first half of the first column *(er)* is **easy** (e / es / e sounds like "easy"). The second column *(re)* is **so so difficult (s s d)**. The third column *(ir)* is the LAST (th**is is it**). The second half of each (nous, vous, ils/elles) is **ons ez ent** every time, except for the last column where your batteries are running out, you're slowing down and you're adding sleepy snoring sounds to it **issons issez issent**.

jouer – to play	répondre – to answer	finir – to finish
je joue tu joues il/elle/on joue nous jouons vous jouez ils/elles jouent	je réponds tu réponds il/elle/on répond nous répondons vous répondez ils/elles répondent	je finis tu finis il/elle/on finit nous finissons vous finissez ils/elles finissent
similar verbs: *écouter – to listen* *habiter – to live* *manger – to eat* *parler – to speak* *aimer – to like* *aider – to help* *chanter – to sing* *dessiner – to draw* *nager – to swim* *danser – to dance* *laver – to wash* *ranger – to tidy* *porter – to wear* *bavarder – to chat* *voyager – to travel*	similar verbs: *vendre – to sell* *descendre – to go down* *entendre – to hear*	similar verbs: *vomir – to be sick* *choisir – to choose*

Now complete the table below

jouer – to play	répondre – to answer	finir – to finish
je jou tu jou il/elle/on jou nous jou vous jou ils/elles jou similar verbs:	je répond tu répond il/elle/on répond nous répond vous répond ils/elles répond similar verbs:	je fin tu fin il/elle/on fin nous fin vous fin ils/elles fin similar verbs:

Test on present tense regular verbs

1. We are playing
2. You (s) go down
3. We choose
4. They tidy
5. She is chatting
6. He sells
7. You (pl) begin
8. I am listening
9. We live
10. She is living
11. I am speaking
12. I speak
13. Lessons begin
14. My brother is watching
15. We play
16. They are chatting
17. My friend is helping
18. My mother travels
19. We finish

Answers

1. We are playing — nous jouons
2. You (s) go down — tu descends
3. We choose — nous choisissons
4. They tidy — ils rangent
5. She is chatting — elle bavarde
6. He sells — il vend
7. You (pl) begin — vous commencez
8. I am listening — j'écoute
9. We live — nous habitons
10. She is living — elle habite
11. I am speaking — je parle
12. I speak — je parle
13. Lessons begin — les cours commencent
14. My brother is watching — mon frère regarde
15. We play — nous jouons
16. They are chatting — ils bavardent
17. My friend is helping — mon ami aide
18. My mother travels — ma mère voyage
19. We finish — nous finissons

Translate into English – note the "little words!

1. Je mange **des** frites / bonbons / céréales / pâtes

2. Nous jouons **au** foot / tennis / rugby

3. Elle regarde **la** télé

4. Il bavarde **avec ses** amis / parents

5. Tu écoutes **de la** musique

6. Je prends **mon** petit déjeuner

7. Il prend **son** dîner

8. Tu prends **ton** déjeuner

9. Je mange **du** pain avec **du** fromage

10. Elle utilise **son** portable

11. Vous aimez **les** chiens?

12. Tu habites **en** France

13. Je range **ma** chambre

14. Il mange **beaucoup de** pizza

Here are the answers. Now put them back into French, checking with previous page.

1. I eat chips

2. We play football

3. She watches television

4. He chats / is chatting with his friends

5. You listen to music

6. I have my breakfast

7. He has his dinner

8. You have your lunch

9. I eat bread and cheese

10. She uses her phone

11. Do you like dogs?

12. You live in France

13. I tidy my room

14. He eats lots of pizza

Irregular verbs in the present tense

There are a lot of irregular verbs in French but here are some of the most useful. Get used to these pairs and groups of verbs being friends – then when you know one, you'll remember the other more easily. The words in bold rhyme.

	faire – to do	aller – to go
Je	fais	vais
Tu	fais	vas
Il	fait	va
Nous	faisons	allons
Vous	faites	allez
Ils	font	vont

	devoir – to have to	boire – to drink	recevoir – to receive
Je	**dois**	**bois**	**reçois**
Tu	**dois**	**bois**	**reçois**
Il	**doit**	**boit**	**reçoit**
Nous	devons	buvons	recevons
Vous	devez	buvez	recevez
Ils	**doivent**	**boivent**	**reçoivent**

	vouloir – to want	pouvoir – to be able to
Je	**veux**	**peux**
Tu	**veux**	**peux**
Il	**veut**	**peut**
Nous	voulons	pouvons
Vous	voulez	pouvez
Ils	**veulent**	**peuvent**

More irregular verbs

1 **jeter / appeler** throw / call	2 **de- /venir/tenir** (be)come / hold	3 **Com- /prendre** Take / understand
Je jette / j'appelle Tu jettes / appelles Il jette / appelle Nous jetons / appelons Vous jetez / appelez Ils jettent / appellent	je viens/tiens tu viens/tiens il vient/tient nous venons/tenons vous venez/tenez ils viennent/tiennent	je (com)prends tu (com)prends il (com)prend nous (com)prenons vous (com)prenez ils (com)prennent
4 **acheter** to buy	5 **voir / croire** to see / believe	6 **sortir/partir/dormir** go out / leave / sleep
j'achète tu achètes il achète nous achetons vous achetez ils achètent	je vois / crois tu vois / crois il voit / croit voyons / croyons voyez / croyez ils voient / croient	pars / sors / dors pars / sors / dors part / sort / dort partons / sortons partez / sortez partent / sortent
7 **dire / lire / conduire** to say, read, drive	8 **(per)mettre** to put (allow)	9 **(d)écrire** to write (describe)
Je dis / lis / conduis Tu dis / lis / conduis Il dit / lit / / conduit disons/lisons/conduisons dites / lisez / conduisez disent/ lisent/conduisent	Je (per)mets Tu (per)mets Il (per)met Nous (per)mettons Vous (per)mettez Ils (per)mettent	J'(d)écris tu (d)écris il (d)écrit nous (d)écrivons vous (d)écrivez ils (d)écrivent

How to remember your irregular verbs

Group 1 – jeter, appeler, rappeler, projeter etc
These take a double consonant in all forms except *nous* and *vous* – another example of this '1236 format' is the *devoir* group and the *vouloir* group above.

Group 2 – venir, revenir, devenir
These follow a pattern along the lines of 1236 above but with the extra i before the e in those forms of the verb, which disappears in *nous* and *vous*. 1236 have the i but 4 and 5 do not. Note the double n in 3rd person plural as well. I remember it as *"come to Vienna"*.

Group 3 – prendre (also: comprendre, apprendre)
With to <u>take</u>, you <u>take</u> out the d for the second half, and like *venir*, a double n in the *ils* form. Venir and prendre have rhyming last lines.

Group 4 – acheter, (also: se lever)
Here the 1236 relates to a grave accent which disappears in *nous* and *vous* forms. So 4 and 5 are accent-less.

Group 5 – voire, croire
Here the 1236 relates to an i which is replaced by a y in *nous* /*vous*.

Group 6 – partir, sortir, dormir
This is the teenager group - all teenagers do is go out, sleep, and leave. Where do they go out of? The doors (*dors*). Once you have the word *dors*, you have *pars* and *sors*, and the rest follows.

Group 7 – conduire, lire, dire (also: construire, détruire, réduire)
The single s in the plural forms sounds like a z, and could be the noise of the car engine. (*conduire* means *drive…*)

Group 8 – mettre, (also: permettre, promettre)
This is tricky to find a technique for, but once you have mastered *je mets la table* for *I lay the table,* the rest should follow

Group 9 – écrire, décrire
If you write something which is *right*, you get a *tick which is shaped* like a v in *écrivons, écrivez, écrivent*

Faire and aller – use with activities

If it's a **game** that you can win use **jouer au** (**aux** for plural)

Je joue au tennis
Je joue au netball
Je joue au basket
Je joue aux cartes / aux échecs / aux jeux-vidéo

With **instruments** it's **jouer du or de la**

Je joue du piano   (« du du du » goes the piano)
Je joue de la guitare   (« la la la » singing to the guitar)

Use **faire du** with masculine activities: Je fais…

du sport	sport
du vélo / VTT	cycling
du patinage	skating
du ski (nautique)	skiing / water skiing
du jogging	jogging

Use **faire de la** if it's feminine (mostly in the **sea**): Je fais…

de la natation	swimming
de la voile	sailing
de la planche à voile	windsurfing
de la plongée	diving
de la gymnastique	gymnastics
de la danse	dance

If it begins with a **vowel** use **faire de l'**

Je fais de l'équitation   I go horseriding
Il fait de l'athlétisme   He does athletics

If you do lots of them, like walks, **faire des**

Elle fait des promenades   She goes for walks
On a fait des randonnées   We went hiking

Practise irregular verbs

1. We do sport every day

2. I go swimming at the weekend

3. He goes cycling sometimes

4. They play tennis in the summer

5. I take out the rubbish

6. We have our breakfast

7. My grandparents come

8. We have to wear a uniform (use *on*)

9. We can't use phones in class

10. I have to do my homework

11. I want to become a teacher

12. We do our homework

Answers

1. Nous faisons du sport tous les jours

2. Le week-end, je fais de la natation

3. Il fait du vélo de temps en temps

4. En été ils jouent au tennis

5. Je sors la poubelle

6. Nous prenons notre petit déjeuner

7. Mes grands-parents viennent

8. On doit porter un uniforme

9. On ne peut pas utiliser les portables en classe

10. Je dois faire mes devoirs

11. Je veux devenir professeur

12. Nous faisons nos devoirs

Describing your home

> **Top tip: Mum owns the house, car, road, the whole town...**
> Notice that all the rooms in the house, and a lot of the things around the house are **feminine** (house, door, window, car, shelves, wardrobe, TV). Imagine that the only place Dad is allowed is the office and sitting room – and garden. He can also have a bed, a computer, a pen and a few other bits (see second list below) but he has to do the housework (le ménage).

Feminine words

une cuisine	a kitchen
une salle à manger	a dining room
une salle de bains	a bathroom
une chambre	a bedroom
une véranda	a conservatory
une table	a table
une armoire	a wardrobe *(for your armour)*
une étagère	a bookshelf *(étages - floors)*
une chaise	a chair
une porte	a door
une fenêtre	a window
une lampe	a lamp
une commode	a chest of drawers
une piscine	a swimming pool
une machine à laver	a washing machine
une cuisinière	a cooker
une télévision	a TV

une Xbox / Playstation	Xbox / Playstation
une ville	a town
une rue	a road

Picture Dad in these rooms only

un salon	a sitting room
un jardin	a garden
un grenier	an attic
un bureau	an office

He can sit on

un canapé	a sofa
un fauteuil	an armchair
un lit	a bed

Daily routine

Je me réveille	I wake up
Je me lève	I get up
Je me douche	I shower
Je me brosse les dents	I brush my teeth
Je m'habille	I get dressed
Je descends	I go downstairs
Je prends mon petit déjeuner	I have my breakfast
Je vais au collège	I go to school
Je rentre chez moi	I go home
Je fais mes devoirs	I do my homework
en regardant la télé	while watching TV
Je fais la grasse matinée	I have a lie-in
Je sors avec mes amis	I go out with my friends
Je me détends	I relax

Jobs around the house

pour gagner	in order to earn
mon argent de poche	my pocket money
Je passe l'aspirateur	I vacuum
Je fais la vaisselle	I wash up *(think: vessels)*
Je lave la voiture	I wash the car *(think : lather)*
Je range ma chambre	I tidy my room
Je prépare le dîner	I make dinner
Je mets la table	I lay the table *(think : meh)*
Je débarrasse la table	I clear the table
Je sors les poubelles	I take the rubbish out
Je ne fais rien	I don't do anything
Je n'ai pas le temps	I don't have time
Ils nous donnent	they give us
trop de devoirs	too much homework
plus important	more important
mon brevet	GCSE equivalent
Je suis en train de	I'm in the middle of

Describing your town

ma ville	my town
mon village	my village
ma région	my region
mon quartier	my neighbourhood
j'y habite depuis 5 ans	I've lived there 5 years
la meilleure région	the best region
à mon avis	in my opinion
ce que j'aime	what I like

c'est qu'il y a	is that there is
tout ce dont j'ai besoin	everything I need
où on peut	where one can
le cinéma (je vais au cinéma)	cinema
le restaurant	restaurant
le collège	school
le parc	park
le café	cafe
le centre commercial	shopping centre
le centre sportif	sports centre
le coiffeur	hairdresser *(quiff)*
le supermarché	supermarket

> **Top tip: Feminine places in town – think holiday:** *go to the bank for money, the library for books, the station to get the train, to the pool, beach, ice rink, then post office to send a postcard.*

la banque (je vais à la banque)	bank
la bibliothèque	library
la gare	station
la piscine	pool
la plage	beach
la patinoire	ice rink
la poste	post office

Transport

*All transport that has an **en**gine uses "en"*

en voiture	by car
en avion	by plane

en bus   by bus
en bateau   by boat
en car   by coach
à pied / à vélo   on foot / by bike

On foot and bike, your legs hurt – ah!

How much can you remember?

1. Name 5 masculine places in the town
2. Name 5 feminine places in the town
3. What gender are most rooms (and things) in the house?
4. Describe your daily routine
5. Name 3 jobs you do in the house
6. Which word comes before engine transport?

For your oral and writing

Describing a place

Use the story below to describe your town or your house (or your school). Look at how we are just changing a few words and phrases here and there but keeping the structure the same. You can watch me do this on my YouTube channel Lucy Martin Tuition.

Key to remembering it: Begin with the name or place. Then three adjectives to describe it. Then what I call the 5-point sentence, because the words in bold show you where the level 9 points are. Then say what you like (using où on peut), what you don't like, and how you'd improve it. When asked about what there is for young people / tourists in your town, what's wrong with it, what you'd change, why you like it etc, you can just pick out the right bits of the speech.

Describing your town (also house, school, anything!)

Ma ville s'appelle Wimbledon. C'est grand, moderne et sympa.

J'ai de la **chance** car à mon avis c'est **la meilleure** région de Londres et j'**y** habite **depuis** cinq ans.

Ce que j'aime c'est qu'il y a beaucoup de choses à faire (*or* il y a tout ce dont j'ai besoin) – un cinéma où on peut regarder des films et un centre commercial où on peut faire du shopping. De plus il y a des parcs où on peut jouer au foot et au tennis.

Ce que je n'aime pas, c'est la pollution. Si je pouvais changer quelque chose je voudrais avoir moins de circulation.

My town is called Wimbledon. It's big, modern and nice. I'm lucky because in my opinion it's the best region of London and I've been living there 5 years. What I like is that there are lots of things to do (or everything I need) – a cinema where you can watch films and a shopping centre where you can go shopping. What I don't like is the pollution. If I could change something, I'd like to have less traffic.

Describing your house (same pattern)

Ma maison se trouve à Wimbledon. C'est grand, moderne et sympa. J'ai de la chance car à mon avis c'est la meilleure maison de mon quartier et j'y habite depuis cinq ans. Ce que j'aime c'est qu'il y a beaucoup de choses à faire (*or* il y a tout ce dont j'ai besoin) – un salon où on peut regarder la télé et un jardin où on peut jouer au foot. Ce que je n'aime pas, c'est que ma chambre est trop petite. Si c'était plus grand je serais content.

My house is in Wimbledon. It's big, modern and nice. I'm lucky because in my opinion it's the best house in my neighbourhood and I've been living there 5 years. What I like is that there are lots of things to do (or everything I need) – a sitting room where you can watch TV and a garden where you can play football. What I don't like is that my room is too small. If it was bigger I would be happy.

Describing your school (same pattern again but note *le meilleur*)

Mon collège se trouve à Wimbledon. C'est grand, moderne et sympa. J'ai de la chance car à mon avis c'est le meilleur collège de Londres et j'y vais depuis cinq ans. Ce que j'aime c'est qu'il y a beaucoup de choses à faire (*or* il y a tout ce dont j'ai besoin) – un terrain de sport où on peut jouer au foot et une bibliothèque où on peut faire les devoirs. Ce que je n'aime pas, c'est que les profs nous donnent trop de devoirs. De plus, les règles sont trop strictes et on est obligé de porter un uniforme. S'il n'y avait pas d'uniforme je serais plus content.

My school is in Wimbledon. It's big, modern and nice. I'm lucky because in my opinion it's the best school in London and I've been going there for 5 years. What I like is that there are lots of things to do (or everything I need) – a sports ground where you can play football and a library where you can do homework. What I don't like is that the teachers give us too much homework. Also the rules are too strict and we have to wear a uniform. If there wasn't a uniform I'd be happier.

Routine (include *après avoir mangé* and *en regardant la télé*)
Le matin, je me lève, je me douche, je me brosse les dents, je m'habille, je descends et puis je prends mon petit déjeuner. Après avoir mangé je quitte la maison. A quatre heures je rentre chez moi, je fais mes devoirs, je prends mon dîner en regardant la télé et après avoir mangé je me couche.

In the morning I get up, have a shower, clean my teeth, get dressed, go downstairs and then I have my breakfast. After eating I leave the house. At 4 I come home, do my homework, have my dinner watching TV and after eating I go to bed.

Transport in your region On peut prendre le bus, le train, le métro, le tramway et les vélos municipaux qui se trouvent partout. Il suffit de s'enregistrer et on peut prendre un vélo et le déposer ailleurs. Moi je m'en sers tous les jours, pour aller au collège, chez des amis, en ville, quoi que ce soit. Mon moyen de transport préféré c'est le bus, parce que je vois tout qui se passe autour de moi. En plus c'est pratique, rapide et facile à utiliser.

You can take the bus, train, underground, tram and community bikes which are everywhere. You just have to register and you can take a bike and drop it off elsewhere. I use them every day to go to school, to friends' houses, into town, whatever. My favourite mode of transport is the bus because I see everything that's going on around me. Also it's practical, fast and easy to use.

Helping at home Pour aider à la maison je range ma chambre de temps en temps, je fais la vaisselle et je mets la table, mais je ne fais pas beaucoup parce que normalement j'ai trop de devoirs qui sont plus importants, surtout juste avant les examens.

To help at home I tidy my room sometimes, I do the washing up and I lay the table, but I don't do much because normally I have too much homework which is more important, especially just before the exams.

NOTES

Day 3

In this session you will be revising:

- Direct and indirect object pronouns
- Vocabulary on the topic of health and hobbies
- Oral and written answers on health

Pronouns

Pronouns stand in the place of nouns. Instead of repeating "my friend Sarah" every time, we use the word "she". When we know what or who we are talking about, we substitute the names of people and objects with words like *he, she, they, it, them, him, her, us, you* etc.

Subject pronouns

Subject pronouns in French are the ones you see in every verb table:

je	I
tu	you (singular)
il	he (or *it*, with masculine nouns)
elle	she (or *it*, with feminine nouns)
on	we / one
nous	we
vous	you (plural)
ils	they (masculine)
elles	they (feminine)

Test yourself on subject pronouns

1. I eat pizza — Je mange de la pizza
2. She goes to France — Elle va en France
3. We cycle — Nous faisons du vélo
4. They (m) watch TV — Ils regardent la télé
5. He went to the station — Il est allé à la gare

Direct object pronouns

If I say, "I like *it / him*", we need to know how to say *it* or *him*, which is the object pronoun because it stands in the place of the object of the sentence.

me	me
te	you
le	him (or *it* with masculine nouns)
la	her (or *it* with feminine nouns)

nous	us
vous	you
les	them

Examples

Je le vois	I see him / it
Il l'aime	he likes it / him / her
Tu la manges	you eat it
Elle le sait	she knows it
Je les adore	I love them
Il t'aide	he helps you
On le fait	we do it

Test yourself on direct object pronouns

1. He hates <u>me</u> — il me déteste
2. He is going to watch <u>you</u> — il va te / vous regarder
3. I see <u>him</u> — je le vois
4. We want <u>her</u> — nous la voulons
5. They bought <u>it</u> — ils l'ont acheté
6. You know <u>us</u> — vous nous connaissez
7. She eats <u>them</u> — elle les mange
8. You do <u>it</u> — tu le fais

Test yourself on subject and direct object pronouns

1. He likes me — Il m'aime
2. They (m) hate her — Ils la détestent
3. They (f) eat them — Elles les mangent
4. You (pl) know them — Vous les connaissez
5. I admire him — Je l'admire
6. We are watching you (pl) — Nous vous regardons

Indirect object pronouns

Some verbs like donner, dire and demander take an indirect object. Indirect object pronouns are the same as direct object pronouns except *le* and *la* become **lui** (meaning *to* him or her) and *les* becomes **leur** (meaning *to* them).

Examples

Ils lui donnent le livre	They give him/her the book
Elle leur dit bonjour	She says hello to them
Je lui donne le crayon	I give him/her the pencil
Il me demande de partir	He asks me to go

Position of pronouns

The object pronoun goes before the verb, and in the past tense before the auxiliary. In the case of the near future tense, or where a modal verb is being used, the pronoun goes before the infinitive.

Examples

Il les mange	He eats them
Nous l'avons bu	We drank it
Je vais le faire	I'm going to do it
Il doit le porter	He has to wear it

Practise subject and indirect object pronouns

1.	I give her the book	je lui donne le livre
2.	I ask him to leave	je lui demande de partir
3.	I tell them the truth	Je leur dis la vérité
4.	He gives her the bread	Il lui donne le pain
5.	She gives them the clothes	Elle leur donne les vêtements

Pronoun "y" meaning *"there"*

Y is the pronoun that you will see replacing an inanimate noun where the verb takes **à**.

aller	je vais à la banque	j'y vais
habiter	j'habite à Londres	j'y habite
jouer	je joue au tennis	j'y joue
penser	je pense aux vacances	j'y pense
retourner	je retourne à la maison	j'y retourne
s'intéresser	je m'intéresse à la politique	je m'y intéresse

Practise y

I am thinking about it	J'y pense
She's been living here ages	Elle y habite depuis longtemps
I go there every day	J'y vais tous les jours
They go there together	Ils y vont ensemble
They are going to go there	Ils vont y aller
I have *been* playing it for 10 years	J'y joue depuis dix ans
I have been living there 2 months	J'y habite depuis deux mois

Pronoun "en" meaning *'of it'* or *'about it'*

En is the pronoun that replaces a noun where that noun follows *de, du, des.* En therefore has a direct "relationship" with verbs that are followed by de

avoir besoin **de**	to need (j'en ai besoin = I need it)
parler **de**	to talk about

AND with many other verbs which are commonly followed by the indefinite articles *du, de la* or *des*

Avoir (du pain / de la glace / des amis)   J'en ai
Manger (du pain / de la glace / des pâtes)   J'en mange
Faire (du vélo, des promenades)   J'en fais
Vouloir (du pain / de la glace / de l'argent)   J'en veux
Ecouter (de la musique, des CDs)   J'en écoute

Turn the noun into *en* in these sentences – cover up the French and test yourself

1. Je mange de la pizza   J'en mange (I eat it)
2. Je fais du sport   J'en fais (I do it)
3. J'ai des amis   J'en ai (I've got some)
4. Je voudrais des lapins   J'en voudrais (I'd like some)
5. Il parle des dangers   Il en parle (talks about them)

Vocabulary

Health

La santé	health
garder la forme	to keep fit
rester en bonne santé	to stay healthy
il faut / on doit	one must
manger sainement	to eat healthily
manger équilibré	eat a balanced diet
s'entraîner	to train
faire du sport	to do sport
éviter le sucre	to avoid sugar
la malbouffe	junk food
bien que ce soit bon	although it's tasty
bouger	to move around
je fais un régime	I'm on a diet
il ne faut pas	one should not
ça fait grossir	it makes you fat
fumer	to smoke
se droguer	to take drugs
boire de l'alcool	to drink alcohol
devenir accro	to get addicted
déprimé	depressed
prévenir	to prevent

de graves maladies	serious illnesses
l'obésité	obesity
le sida	AIDS
de plus en plus de	more and more
le cancer de poumons	lung cancer
les crises cardiaques	heart attacks
des comprimés	pills
tousser	to cough
j'ai mal à la tête / au bras	my head / arm hurts
je me suis cassé la jambe	I broke my leg
un rhume	a cold
je suis enrhumé	I have a cold
la grippe	flu

Body

le bras	arm

*(think: flex your biceps to show you are **bra**ve)*

la jambe	leg

*(think: messy breakfast-eater drops **jam** on leg)*

la tête	head

(think: the accent is like a little hat on a head)

les oreilles	ears

*(think: hear people shout "**ooray!**")*

les épaules	shoulders

(think: "hey Paul!" you slap his shoulder…)

le nez	nose

*(think: horse with long nose saying "**neigh**")*

les dents	teeth
*(think: **dent**ist)*	
le dos (pronounced "doh")	back
*(think: **back door** sounds like back – dos)*	
la main	hand
*(think: the **main thing** you need to do anything)*	
le pied	foot
*(think: « **pied**estrian »)*	
la bouche	mouth
les yeux	eyes
le ventre / l'estomac	stomach
les genoux	knees
les joues	cheeks
la cheville	ankle

Sports and hobbies

jouer au foot, rugby, cricket	to play football etc
jouer aux échecs	to play chess
jouer aux cartes	to play cards
jouer à l' ordinateur	to play on computer
jouer à la Xbox	to play Xbox
jouer du piano	to play piano
jouer du violon	to play violin
jouer de la guitare	to play guitar
jouer de la clarinette	to play clarinet
jouer de la batterie	to play drums

faire du sport	to do/play sport
faire du patinage	to go skating
faire du vélo / cyclisme	to go cycling
faire du VTT	to go mountain biking
faire du shopping	to go shopping
faire du skate	to skateboard
faire du ski	to ski
faire du ski-nautique	to waterski
faire du jardinage	to do gardening
faire du bricolage	to do DIY
faire du camping	to go camping

Activities - feminine

> *Top tip: Beach scene for feminine activities*
>
> *(Imagine you are swimming and people are sailing, windsurfing, diving, and on the beach doing gym, weights and dancing...)*

faire de la natation	to go swimming
faire de la voile	to go sailing
faire de la planche à voile	to windsurf *(plank sail)*
faire de la plongée	to do diving *(plunge)*
faire de la gymnastique	to do gymnastics
faire de la danse	to dance
faire de la musculation	to do weight training

and if it begins with a vowel "faire de l'"

faire de l'équitation	to go horseriding

faire de l'athlétisme	to do athletics
faire de l'escrime	to do fencing *(scream!)*
faire de l'escalade	to go climbing *(escalator)*
faire de l'alpinisme	to go mountaineering *(alps)*

and if it's plural "faire des"

faire des promenades	to go for walks
faire des randonnées	to go hiking

Other activities

J'aime la lecture	I like reading
lire	to read
aller à la pêche	to go fishing
faire du camping	to go camping
collectionner	to collect
des timbres	stamps
dessiner	to draw
chanter	to sing
danser	to dance
tricoter	to knit
les loisirs	leisure activities
le centre de loisirs	leisure centre

Cinema and TV

le dernier film que j'ai vu	the last film I saw
il s'agit de	it's about
je l'aime	I like it
je l'ai aimé	I liked it

ça me fait rire	it makes me laugh
passionnant	exciting
mon émission préférée	my favourite show
je le trouve	I find it
les dessins animés	cartoons
les actualités / les infos	the news
quotidien	daily
hebdomadaire	weekly
les feuilletons	soaps
les documentaires	documentaries
la téléréalité	reality TV
les jeux télévisés	game shows
la chaîne	channel
l'écran	screen
les téléspectateurs	viewers
les auditeurs	listeners
les vedettes	film stars
la zapette	the remote control
les films romantiques	romantic films
les films d'action	action films
les films d'horreur	horror films
les films de guerre	war films
les films de science-fiction	sci fi films
les films d'aventures	adventure films
les films policiers	detective films

How much can you remember?

Which are the three main verbs that take an indirect object?

What is the rule about the position of pronouns?

Name as many body parts as you can, with their gender.

For your oral and writing

Sport and hobbies Je suis accro au sport parce que c'est amusant, énergique et bon pour la santé physique et mentale. Je joue au tennis deux fois par semaine. J'ai de la chance parce que je suis membre d'un club de tennis depuis cinq ans et je fais partie de l'équipe scolaire. En plus je joue au foot et au rugby et je fais de l'athlétisme. Pendant les vacances je fais du vélo avec mon père.

I'm addicted to sport because it's fun, energetic and good for your physical and mental health. I play tennis twice a week. I'm lucky because I have been a member of a tennis club for five years and I am in my school team. I also play football and rugby and I do athletics. During the holidays I go cycling with my father.

How to stay healthy Il faut considérer la santé mentale aussi bien que la santé physique. Pour rester en forme il faut manger plein de légumes et de fruits, il faut boire huit verres d'eau par jour et il faut éviter le sucre et la matière grasse, et bien sûr l'alcool et le tabac. Il faut faire de l'exercice et passer du temps en plein air. C'est bon non seulement pour garder la forme mais aussi pour remonter le moral et les sports d'équipe ont un bon effet sur l'esprit.

You have to consider mental as well as physical health. To stay healthy you have to eat lots of vegetables and fruit, you have to drink 8 glasses of water a day and avoid sugar and fat, and of course alcohol and tobacco. You should do exercise and spend time in the fresh air. It's good not only for keeping fit but also for cheering you up and team sports have a good effect on the spirit.

How you stay healthy Pour moi c'est important de rester en forme et de rester content et positif. Donc je mange sainement et j'essaie d'éviter le sucre et la matière grasse, mais ce n'est pas toujours facile car j'adore le chocolat. En plus je bois un litre d'eau par jour, je dors huit heures par nuit et je m'entraîne au gymnase tous les jours.

Je n'ai jamais fumé et je n'aime pas l'alcool. Peut-être que ça changera à l'avenir mais j'ai de bonnes intentions!

It's important to me to keep fit and to stay happy and positive. So I eat healthily and I try to avoid sugar and fat but it's not always easy as I love chocolate. I also drink a litre of water a day, I sleep 8 hours a night and I train at the gym every day. I have never smoked and I don't like alcohol. Maybe that will change in the future but I have good intentions!

Sickness J'ai de la chance parce que je ne tombe malade que très rarement. Normalement si ce n'est pas grave, il faut rester au lit mais si tu ne vas pas mieux après quelques jours il faut aller chez le médecin, qui te donnera des médicaments.

I'm lucky because I only very rarely get ill. Normally if it's not serious you have to stay in bed but if you're not better after a few days you have to go to the doctor who will give you medicines.

Smoking (adapt for alcohol and drugs) Fumer c'est ridicule, car on sait que ça raccourcit la vie et ça entraîne de graves maladies comme le cancer. Je ne fumerai jamais. Je pense que les ados commencent à fumer pour de diverses raisons. La raison principale c'est la pression du groupe. Si on va à une soirée il y a toujours des ados qui fument sans que leurs parents ne le sachent et il y aura toujours des autres qui veulent faire partie du groupe, mais moi non.

Smoking is ridiculous as we know it shortens your life and causes serious illnesses like cancer. I will never smoke. I think young people start smoking for a variety of reasons. The main reason is peer pressure. If you go to a party there are always teenagers smoking without their parents' knowledge and there will always be others who want to be part of the group, but not me.

NOTES

Day 4

In this session you will be revising:
- The past tense (passé composé) with avoir
- The past tense (passé composé) with être
- Vocabulary relating to food and shopping
- Oral and written answers on past events

The past tense (passé composé)

To form this tense, which is used to talk about past events, use the person, auxiliary and past participle.

The person is the subject of the verb and can be a person's name or a pronoun that represents it.

The auxiliary is the present tense of avoir or être.

The past participle follows this rule: *Verbs ending in -er go to é*
Verbs ending in -re go to u
Verbs ending in -ir go to i

Examples

Ils ont joué au foot	They played football
Nous avons ecouté le prof	We listened to the teacher
Mon père a vendu la maison	My father sold the house
J'ai entendu le bruit	I heard the noise
Sandrine a choisi ses amis	Sandrine chose her friends
Je suis allé à la banque	I went to the bank
Jean est arrivé à midi	Jean arrived at midday.

Most verbs take the auxiliary *avoir* in the past tense but a certain number take *être*. (See the last two examples above.)

So how do we know which auxiliary to use? Some schools teach *Dr/Mrs Vandertramp* as a mnemonic for this list, and there are some reasons to use it, for example you can quickly establish that a verb like *quitter* does not take *être* because there is no Q in the mnemonic at all, but if you are given a verb like *rester* or *ranger,* how do you establish quickly whether or not it is one of the Rs in the mnemonic? This is why I prefer the image of the house on the next page. When you are having to conjugate a verb in the past tense, just picture this house and ask yourself: Is that verb in the house?

Verbs that take être (house verbs and bedroom verbs)

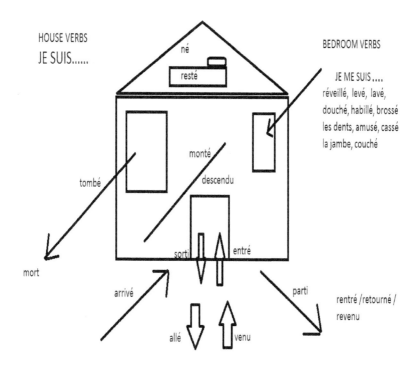

The difference between these verbs and the ones that take **avoir** is that with these, *the past participle must agree* with the subject of the verb (the person that did it) in gender and number. Add *e* for feminine and *s* for plural. For example:

elle est tombée	she fell
nous sommes arrivées	we (fem plural) arrived
ils sont partis	they left (masc plural)
vous êtes sortis	you (masc plural) went out
nous sommes allés	we (masc plural) went

Irregular past participles

Finally, when it comes to forming the past participle, there is a list of exceptions to the general rule. Here are the main ones:

avoir	--> J'ai eu	I had
boire	--> J'ai bu	I drank
croire	--> J'ai cru	I believed
devoir -	--> J'ai dû	I had to
savoir	--> J'ai su	I knew (fact)
voir	--> J'ai vu	I saw
pouvoir	--> J'ai pu	I was able to
connaître	--> J'ai connu	I knew (person)
lire	--> J'ai lu	I read
venir	--> Je suis venu	I came
vouloir	--> J'ai voulu	I wanted
courir	--> J'ai couru	I ran
recevoir	--> J'ai reçu	I received
vivre	--> J'ai vécu	I lived
prendre -	--> J'ai pris	I took
apprendre -	--> J'ai appris	I learnt
comprendre	--> J'ai compris	I understood
mettre	--> J'ai mis	I put
dire	--> J'ai dit	I said
écrire	--> J'ai écrit	I wrote
conduire	--> J'ai conduit	I drove
construire	--> J'ai construit	I built
ouvrir	--> J'ai ouvert	I opened
faire	--> J'ai fait	I did / made
être	--> J'ai été	I was
naître	--> Je suis né	I was born
mourir	--> il est mort	he died

Test yourself on the past tense

1. We went (m) on holiday
2. We went (f) to the countryside
3. I went to the cinema
4. I went to the beach
5. They (f) went to the pool
6. He had to do his homework
7. She received lots of presents
8. I saw my friend at the station
9. I built a house in France
10. The teachers drank lots of wine
11. We had our breakfast
12. She stayed in London
13. She left last weekend
14. My brother listened to music
15. My mother watched the television
16. I went cycling
17. She went swimming
18. My parents played tennis

Answers

1. Nous sommes partis / allés en vacances
2. Nous sommes allées à la campagne
3. Je suis allé(e) au cinéma
4. Je suis allé(e) à la plage
5. Elles sont allées à la piscine
6. Il a dû faire ses devoirs
7. Elle a reçu beaucoup de cadeaux
8. J'ai vu mon ami à la gare
9. J'ai construit une maison en France
10. Les profs ont bu beaucoup de vin
11. Nous avons pris notre petit déjeuner
12. Elle est restée à Londres
13. Elle est partie le week-end dernier
14. Mon frère a écouté de la musique
15. Ma mère a regardé la télévision
16. J'ai fait du vélo / cyclisme
17. Elle a fait de la natation
18. Mes parents ont joué au tennis

Vocabulary

> ***Top tip***: *The food I ate today is un, une, du de la or des*

Un / une – if you eat / drink / want the whole thing

Most fruit is feminine, so imagine ladies eating fruit

une poire	pear
une pomme	apple
une banane	banana
une pêche	peach
une orange	orange
une mandarine	satsuma
une mangue	mango
une pastèque	watermelon
une cerise	cherry
une fraise	strawberry
une framboise	raspberry
une prune	plum

Except

un ananas	a pineapple
un melon	a melon
un pamplemousse	a grapefruit
un abricot	an apricot

Remember that if you eat fruit in the plural, use *des*

Je mange des framboises — I eat raspberries

Stodgy food, spirits and hot drinks FOR MEN!

un œuf	an egg
un croissant	a croissant
un pain au chocolat/raisin	a pastry
un biscuit	a biscuit
un gâteau	a cake
un sandwich	a sandwich
un chocolat chaud	a hot chocolate
un café	a coffee
un thé	a tea
un whisky	a whisky
(except *un* jus d'orange	an orange juce)

Du - with masculine foods – think PICNIC

du pain	bread
du vin	wine
du boursin	(a type of french cheese)
du beurre	butter (bu- - er)
du fromage	cheese
du poulet	chicken
du jambon	ham
du canard	duck
du saucisson	sausage
du salami	salami
du bœuf	beef
du porc	pork
du poisson	fish
du thon	tuna
du cabillaud	cod

du pâté	pâté
du gâteau	cake
du chocolat	chocolate
du sel	salt
du miel	honey
du sucre	sugar
du lait	milk

"De la" - feminine foods are on the RED LIST

de la viande	meat *(red meat)*
de la confiture	jam *(strawberry jam)*
de la glace	ice cream *(strawberry)*
de la pizza	pizza *(tomato pizza)*
de la soupe	soup *(tomato soup)*
de la sauce	sauce *(tomato sauce)*

"De l' if there is some of it and it starts with a vowel

de l'agneau	lamb
de l'eau	water

Plural food – if you eat / have lots, use « des »

des chips	crisps *(not chips !!!!)*
des frites	chips *(fries!)*
des escargots	snails
des céréales	cereal *(plural cereals)*
des pâtes	pasta *(plural pastas)*
des œufs	eggs
des légumes	vegetables
des pommes de terre	potatoes
des carottes	carrots
des petits pois	peas *(little peas)*

des haricots verts	green beans
des champignons	mushrooms *(champions)*
des oignons	onions
des choux de Bruxelles	brussels sprouts
des fruits	fruit
des cerises	cherries
des fraises	strawberries
des framboises	raspberries
des raisins	grapes
des raisins secs	raisins *(dry grapes)*
des saucisses	sausages
des crêpes	pancakes
des bonbons	sweets
des fruits de mer	seafood
des moules	mussels
des crudités	raw vegetables

At the restaurant

j'ai faim	I'm hungry
réserver une table	to book a table
pour commencer	to begin with
comme plat principal	as a main dish
commander	to order
vous avez choisi?	have you chosen?
un repas	meal
l'addition	bill
le plat du jour	dish of the day
les plats régionaux	local dishes

service compris	service included
un pourboire	tip
le serveur	waiter
la serveuse	waitress
Garçon!	waiter!
saignant	rare
à point	medium
bien cuit	well done
le dessert	pudding
je prends	I'll have
Bon appétit!	enjoy your meal!

Shopping

les magasins	the shops
faire les magasins	to go shopping
faire du shopping	to go shopping
faire les courses	to go food shopping
faire des achats	to buy things
acheter	to buy
en ligne	online
le vendeur /euse	shop assistant
l'argent de poche	pocket money
économiser	to save
dépenser	to spend
gaspiller	to waste
un portefeuille	wallet
les soldes	the sales
faire du lèche-vitrine	to go window shopping

How much can you remember?

Name 8 verbs that take être in the passé composé.

When does the past particple agree with the subject?

Give an example of the past participle agreeing.

Name 8 verbs with a past participle that ends in u.

For your oral and writing

Last weekend (use this as a standard story and adapt for the future tense)

Le week-end dernier je suis allé au centre commercial avec mon ami pour acheter un cadeau pour ma mère parce que c'était son anniversaire. J'ai acheté un livre car elle adore la lecture. Puis nous sommes allés au cinéma pour regarder un film d'action. Je les adore car il y a de bons effets spéciaux. En arrivant au cinéma nous avons acheté des billets et des bonbons. Le film était génial et les acteurs ont super-bien joué. Avant de rentrer nous avons mangé dans un restaurant. J'ai pris une pizza, mon ami a pris des frites et pour le dessert nous avons pris de la glace. Après avoir mangé j'ai dû retourner chez moi pour faire mes devoirs.

Last weekend I went to the shopping centre to buy a present for my mother because it was her birthday. I bought a book because she loves reading. Then we went to the cinema to see an action film. I love them because there are good special effects. The film was great and the actors were really convincing. Before going home we ate in a restaurant. I had a pizza, my friend had chips and for pudding we had ice cream. After eating I had to go home to do my homework.

A memorable day (this one you can insert into any story) Un jour j'ai décidé d'organiser un match de foot entre les profs et les élèves / les parents et les enfants pour collecter des fonds pour une association caritative / Oxfam / mon collège / une nouvelle bibliothèque / les SDF. Avant de commencer le match, je suis allé au supermarché pour acheter beaucoup de bonbons et de chocolat. J'ai vendu les bonbons et les parents les ont mangés en regardant le match. Nous avons collecté cent euros pour la bibliothèque et les enfants ont gagné le match. Quelle chance!

One day I decided to organize a football match between the teachers and the pupils to collect funds for a charity. Before the match I went to the supermarket to buy lots of sweets and chocolate. I sold the sweets and the parents ate them while watching the match. We collected 100 euros for the charity and the children won the match. What luck!

Your last birthday Pour fêter mon dernier anniversaire, je suis allée au restaurant avec ma famille et j'ai mangé mon repas préféré, la pizza. C'était super et je me suis bien amusée. Cependant après avoir mangé je suis rentrée chez moi et, quelle désastre – le chien avait mangé mon gâteau d'anniversaire! On a dû aller en chercher un autre au magasin.

To celebrate my last birthday I went to a restaurant with my family and I ate my favourite meal, pizza. It was great and I had a lot of fun. However, after eating, I went home and, what a disaster, the dog had eaten my birthday cake ! We had to go and get another one from the shop.

The last film you saw Le dernier film que j'ai vu était la Mort de Stalin. C'était une comédie, mais je ne l'ai pas trouvé drôle, donc j'ai été un peu déçue. Cependant, j'ai appris quelque chose sur l'histoire de la Russie donc ça a valu la peine d'y aller. Les acteurs ont super-bien joué. J'ai préféré Maze Runner que j'ai vu l'année dernière. J'étais scotché à l'écran jusqu'au dernier moment du film.

The last film I saw was the Death of Stalin. It was a comedy but I didn't find it funny so I was a bit disappointed. However, I learnt something about the history of Russia so it was worth going. The actors were really good. I preferred Maze Runner which I saw last year. I was glued to the screen until the last moment of the film.

The last book you read Le dernier roman que j'ai lu était les jeux de faim. Il s'agit d'enfants qui doivent se battre dans un milieu dangereux dans un jeu télévisé. Les téléspectateurs peuvent leur livrer des cadeaux pour les aider à survivre, et il n'y a qu'un seul gagnant. Tous les autres meurent.

The last book I read was the Hunger Games. It's about children who have to fight in a dangerous environment in a TV show. The TV audience can deliver them presents to help them survive and there is only one winner. All the others die.

French films you have seen J'ai vu un film français qui s'appelle 'Les Choristes', un film de Christophe Barratier. C'est l'histoire d'un prof de musique dans un internat de rééducation. En enseignant le chant choral, il réussit à transformer la vie des garçons. Je l'ai trouvé amusant et triste en même temps.

I saw a French film called "the choristers", a Christophe Barratier film. It's the story of a music teacher in a reform boarding school. By teaching choral singing he manages to transform the lives of the boys. I found it funny and sad at the same time.

French-speaking countries you've been to Je suis allé en France plusieurs fois et je l'ai beaucoup aimée, car le paysage est pittoresque et la cuisine la meilleure du monde. En plus, le climat est plus agréable qu'en Angleterre. Quant aux autres pays francophones, j'en connais, mais je ne les ai pas visités. On parle français aux îles Caraïbes et en Afrique du nord, mais je n'y suis jamais allé.

I've been to France many times and I liked it a lot, as the scenery is picturesque and the food the best in the world. Also, the weather is better than in England. As for other French speaking countries, I do know some, but I haven't been to any. They speak French in the Caribbean and in North Africa, but I've never been there.

Last Christmas L'année dernière toute ma famille est venue chez nous, y compris mes cousins que je ne vois qu'une fois par an. On a mangé un repas splendide, et après avoir regardé le discours de la reine à la télé on a joué aux jeux de société ensemble et on a échangé des cadeaux. J'ai reçu des vêtements et des nouveaux baskets dont j'avais rêvé depuis longtemps. C'était genial.

Last year all my family came to us including my cousins whom I only see once a year. We ate an amazing meal and after watching the Queen's speech we played board games together and exchanged presents. I received clothes and new trainers I'd been dreaming about for ages. It was great.

Yesterday at school Hier j'ai eu une journée parfaite. Je suis arrivé au collège à huit heures et après avoir mis mes affaires dans mon casier, j'ai pris mes cahiers et mes livres pour les deux premiers cours. Puis je suis allé à ma salle de classe et j'ai bavardé avec mes amis. Le prof de maths a annulé notre contrôle et le prof d'anglais était absent. Pendant la pause déjeuner mes copains et moi sommes allés au terrain de sport pour jouer au foot. L'après-midi il n'y avait que deux cours de plus car j'ai dû participer au concours de tennis et heureusement j'ai gagné !

Yesterday I had a perfect day. I arrived at school at 8 and after putting my things in my locker I took my books for the first two lessons. Then I went to my classroom and chatted with my friends. The maths teacher cancelled our test and the English teacher was away. During lunch my friends and I went to the sports field to play football. In the afternoon there were only two more lessons as I had to play in a tennis tournament and luckily I won!

School trips Hier, j'ai eu de la chance car moi et mes amis sommes allés à Londres pour assister à un concert au Festival Hall. C'était un voyage scolaire avec tous mes copains qui étudient la musique. La musique était extraordinaire et je l'ai adorée. Je suis rentré très tard chez moi et le lendemain j'étais très fatigué. J'ai envie d'y retourner parce que ça m'a vraiment inspiré.

Yesterday I was lucky because my friends and I went to London to see a concert at the Festival Hall. It was a school trip with all my friends who study music. The music was extraordinary, and I loved it. I got home very late and the next day I was very tired. I would like to go back there because it really inspired me.

Last year's holiday L'année dernière je suis allé en France en avion avec ma famille. Nous sommes restés dans un hôtel près de la plage pendant quinze jours. Je suis allé à la plage, j'ai joué au tennis avec mon frère, nous avons visité des monuments, j'ai pris des photos et j'ai acheté des cadeaux. De plus, j'ai goûté les plats régionaux comme les escargots. Malheureusement, quand c'était l'heure du départ, j'ai perdu mon passeport et nous avons presque raté l'avion. Heureusement je l'ai trouvé dans ma valise.

Last year I went to France by plane with my family. We stayed in a hotel near the beach for 2 weeks. I went to the beach, I played tennis with my brother, we visited monuments, I took photos and I bought presents. I also tried the local dishes like snails. Unfortunately, when it was time to leave, I lost my passport and we nearly missed the plane. Fortunately I found it in my suitcase.

NOTES

Day 5

In this session you will be revising:

- The imperfect tense
- Vocabulary relating to holidays
- Oral and written answers that use the imperfect tense

The imperfect tense

This is used to describe
- an action in the past that you used to do (**repeated**)
  Quand *j'étais* jeune *je faisais* de la natation tous les jours.
  When *I was* young *I went swimming* every day.

- or when you are stressing the fact that this **WAS going on** rather than the completion of the action
  Je nettoyais la maison quand il est arrivé.
  I was cleaning the house when he arrived.

- or **with the conditional** tense as in English
  Si j'*étais* riche, j'achèterais un bateau.
  If *I was* rich, I would buy a boat.

- or to say "**was going** to" as in English
  J'allais faire mes devoirs, mais j'étais trop fatigué.
  I was going to do my homework but I was too tired.

- To say "it was" (c'était) and "there was" (il y avait)

To make and use the imperfect tense...
Take the nous form of the present tense (eg **jouons**), take the *ons* off and add the endings:

je jou**ais**	I played
tu jou**ais**	you played
il jou**ait**	he played
nous jou**ions**	we played
vous jou**iez**	you played
ils / elles jou**aient**	they played

The only exception is être – where you add the above endings on to « et » because there is no *ons* to take off in the nous form.

Practise the imperfect tense

This is particularly important when describing your childhood, or at the beginning of an *if* sentence.

I used to play tennis	je jouais au tennis
They used to play	ils jouaient au tennis
I went cycling every day	je faisais du vélo tous les jours
I lived in Spain	j'habitais en Espagne
It was great fun	c'était très amusant
I had a dog	j'avais un chien
I didn't have a cat	je n'avais pas de chat
I wanted to have a rabbit	je voulais avoir un lapin
There was a cinema in town	il y avait un cinéma en ville
There wasn't a pool	il n'y avait pas de piscine
I was happy	j'étais content
There was less homework	il y avait moins de devoirs
There were more shops	il y avait plus de magasins
It was smaller	c'était plus petit
If I could change	si je pouvais changer
If I was rich	si j'étais riche
If I had a dog	si j'avais un chien
If there was less pollution	s'il y avait moins de pollution

Vocabulary

On holiday– en vacances

je suis allé	I went
j'ai passé	I spent (time)
quinze jours	a fortnight
au bord de la mer	by the sea
au camping	at the campsite
en montagne	in the mountains
en colonie de vacances	on a holiday camp
en ville	in the city
nous avons logé	we stayed
dans un hôtel	in a hotel
dans une auberge	at a hostel
dans un appartement	in an apartment
dans une gîte	in a gite
à la station balnéaire	at the seaside resort
à la station de ski	at the ski resort
louer	to hire
nous avons loué	we hired
les valises	suitcases
à l'étranger	abroad
j'ai perdu mon passeport	I lost my passport
retardé	delayed
le vol	the flight
a été annulé	was cancelled
J'ai raté l'avion	I missed the plane
il y avait du monde	it was crowded
avec vue sur	with a view over

avec balcon	with a balcony
faire les valises	to pack suitcases
défaire les valises	to unpack
se bronzer	to sunbathe
se détendre	to relax
se reposer	to rest
se baigner	to swim
se souvenir de	to remember
visiter des monuments	to visit monuments
visiter des musées	to visit the museums
prendre des photos	to take photos
goûter les plats régionaux	to sample local dishes
acheter des cadeaux	to buy presents
se faire des amis	to make friends
les sites touristiques	tourist attractions
Il a fait beau	the weather was good
Il a plu deux fois	it rained twice
une canicule	a heatwave
J'ai envie d'y retourner	I'd like to go back there
J'ai hâte d'y aller	I can't wait to go there
le meilleur pays	the best country
J'ai eu de la chance	I was lucky

Trains

le guichet	ticket office
un billet simple	a single ticket
un billet aller-retour	a return ticket
c'est quel quai?	Which platform is it?

le consigne de bagages	left luggage
rater le train	to miss the train
en retard	late
les bagages	luggage
le voyage	journey

Weather

il fait beau	the weather is good
il fait mauvais	the weather is bad
il fait chaud	it's hot
il fait froid	it's cold

*With things you can see or feel, say **il y a** = there is*

il y a du vent	it's windy
il y a du soleil	it's sunny
il y a des nuages	it's cloudy
il y a du brouillard	it's foggy
il y a de la brume	it's misty

And if things are falling out of the sky, use the verb!

il neige	it's snowing
il grêle	it's hailing
il pleut	it's raining

But watch out for irregularities with pleuvoir

il a plu	it rained
il va pleuvoir	it is going to rain
la pluie	rain

More weather terms

il fait un froid de canard	it's freezing
il pleut à verse	it's pouring
des averses	showers
le ciel est couvert	it is overcast *(covered)*
la météo	weather forecast
la chaleur	heat *(from chaud)*
la canicule	heatwave
le tonnerre	thunder *(a tonne in the air)*
un orage	storm *(rage)*
une tempête	storm
un éclair	flash of lightning
des éclaircies	sunny spells
frappé par la foudre	struck by lightning

Time phrases

Il est neuf heures moins le quart	8.45
Il est deux heures et demie	2.30
Il est huit heures et quart	8.15
Il est trois heures vingt	3.20
Il est onze heures moins vingt	10.40
à minuit	at midnight
à midi	at midday
hier	yesterday
demain	tomorrow
après avoir mangé	after eating

de temps en temps	sometimes
tous les jours	every day
le samedi	on Saturdays
la semaine dernière	last week *(note the e on both)*
l'année dernière	last year *(note the e on both)*
le weekend dernier	last weekend *(no e or accent)*
le mois dernier	last month *(no e or accent)*
la semaine prochaine	next week *(note the e on both)*
l'année prochaine	next year *(note the e on both)*

Days of the week

lundi	Monday
mardi	Tuesday
mercredi	Wednesday
jeudi	Thursday
vendredi	Friday *(get the van ready)*
samedi	Saturday
dimanche	Sunday
le week-end	at the weekend

Months of the year *(no capitals in French)*

janvier	January
février	February
mars	March
avril	April
mai	May
juin	June

juillet	July
août	August
septembre	September
octobre	October
novembre	November
décembre	December

Seasons

au printemps	in spring *("oh! it's Spring!")*
en été	in summer
en automne	in autumn
en hiver	in winter
à Pâques	at Easter
à Noël	at Christmas
le Toussaint	All-saints (October half-term)

How much can you remember?

In what circumstances do we use the imperfect tense?

What are the endings of the imperfect?

What is the root we put these endings on?

Which verb is the only exception?

For your oral and writing

Past hobbies Quand j'étais jeune je faisais moins de sport mais je passais mon temps à jouer dans le parc avec mes amis. Je regardais la télévision et je jouais aux jeux de société avec ma famille.

When I was young I played less sport but I spent most of my time playing in the park with my friends. I used to watch TV and play board games with my family.

Your primary school Quand j'étais petit j'allais à une école primaire près de chez moi. C'était plus petit que mon collège et les profs étaient moins stricts. Il n'y avait pas beaucoup de devoirs et j'étais beaucoup moins stressé.

When I was little I went to a primary school near my house. It was smaller than my secondary school and the teachers were less strict. There wasn't much homework and I was much less stressed.

Weekend job (the activities are similar to helping in the house)
L'année dernière j'ai travaillé dans un restaurant pendant les grandes vacances. Je devais préparer les légumes, mettre les tables et servir les repas aux clients. Je nettoyais la cuisine chaque soir aussi. Ce n'était pas bien payé mais je recevais des pourboires tous les jours, donc j'ai pu économiser un peu d'argent.

Last year I worked in a restaurant in the summer holidays. I had to prepare vegetables, lay the tables and serve meals to customers. I cleaned the kitchen every evening too. It wasn't well-paid but I received tips every day so I was able to save a bit of money.

What you would change about your routine
Si je pouvais changer quelque chose, je voudrais me lever plus tard et commencer l'école à midi, car je suis toujours fatigué le matin, et les scientifiques ont prouvé que les ados ont besoin de plus de sommeil le matin.

If I could change something, I would like to get up later and start school at midday as I'm always tired in the mornings, and scientists have proved that teenagers need more sleep in the morning.

Day 6

In this session you will be revising:

- The near future tense
- The simple future tense
- Vocabulary relating to education and jobs
- Oral and written answers on education, jobs and future plans

The near future tense

In English we say, "I am going to eat an apple". We can translate this directly into French: **Je vais manger une pomme** = I am going to eat an apple. Use the present of **aller** followed by the infinitive.

Je vais
Tu vas
Il va
Nous allons
Vous allez
Ils vont

regarder / aller / sortir / faire / finir / répondre

Simple future tense (not so simple)
We can also express the future by saying we *will* do something. This form of the future is made by putting special endings onto (usually) the infinitive. The endings will remind you of the verb avoir.

manger	répondre	finir
je manger**ai**	je répondr**ai**	je finir**ai**
tu manger**as**	tu répondr**as**	tu finir**as**
il manger**a**	il répondr**a**	il finir**a**
nous manger**ons**	nous répondr**ons**	nous finir**ons**
vous manger**ez**	vous répondr**ez**	vous finir**ez**
ils manger**ont**	ils répondr**ont**	ils finir**ont**

The most important irregular future roots

avoir (to have)	j'**aur**ai	I will have
savoir (to know)	je **saur**ai	I will know
être (to be)	je **ser**ai	I will be
faire (to do)	je **fer**ai	I will do
aller (to go)	j'**ir**ai	I will go
pouvoir (to be able to)	je **pourr**ai	I will be able to
devoir (to have to)	je **devr**ai	I will have to
voir (to see)	je **verr**ai	I will see
venir (to come)	je **viendr**ai	I will come
vouloir (to want)	je **voudr**ai	I will want

Test yourself on the future tense

I am going to meet my friends	je vais retrouver mes amis
He is going to go to school	il va aller au collège
They (m) are going to eat	ils vont manger
She is going to play tennis	elle va jouer au tennis
We are going to go out	nous allons sortir
You (s) are going to forget	tu vas oublier
You (pl) are going to begin	vous allez commencer
They (f) are going to win	elles vont gagner
I will go to France	j'irai en France
They will go to London	ils iront à Londres
He will go to the countryside	il ira à la campagne
You (s) will go on holiday	tu iras en vacances
She will do her homework	elle fera ses devoirs
I will go cycling	je ferai du vélo / cyclisme
We will go swimming	nous ferons de la natation
I will have a big house	j'aurai une grande maison
It will be great	ce sera genial
There will be a pool	il y aura une piscine
I will be happy	je serai content
We will have to work	nous devrons travailler
We will be able to play	nous pourrons jouer
When I'm older	quand je serai plus âgé

(this last one is a special case and you need to learn it!)

Vocabulary

School subjects

J'étudie	I study
l'histoire	history
l'informatique	ICT
l'anglais	English
les maths	maths
les sciences	science
le sport	sport
le dessin	art
le français	French
la géographie	geography
la musique	music
l'EPS	PE
ma matière préférée	my favourite subject
Je suis fort(e) en	I'm good at
Je suis nul(le) en	I'm bad at
J'ai de bonnes notes	I get good marks
J'ai de mauvaises notes	I get bad marks
Si je pouvais	if I could
je supprimerais les maths	I'd get rid of maths

The school facilities and routine

dans mon collège	in my school
des salles de classe	classrooms
des laboratoires	laboratories
des terrains de sport	sports fields
une bibliothèque	a library

une cantine	a canteen
une piscine	a pool
la cour	the playground
des contrôles	tests
des examens	exams
un théâtre	theatre
en arrivant	on arriving
un cours	lesson
l'uniforme	the uniform
beaucoup de choses à faire	lots of things to do
j'y vais depuis…	I've been going there for…

Routine

neuf cours par jour	9 lessons a day
chaque cours dure	each lesson lasts
pendant la récréation	during break time
la pause déjeuner	lunch break
les cours devraient	lessons should
commencer plus tard	begin later
les cours finissent	lessons finish
les activités extra-scolaires	after-school clubs
un voyage scolaire	school trip
un échange	an exchange
interne	a boarder
préparer le brevet	to do your GCSEs

School rules

il faut	you have to

obligatoire	compulsory
on peut	one can
facultatif	optional
on ne peut pas	one cannot
avoir le droit de	to be allowed to
on n'a pas le droit de	we're not allowed to
porter des bijoux	to wear jewellery
utiliser les portables	to use mobiles
parler en classe	to talk in lessons
sécher les cours	to bunk off lessons
J'en ai marre	I'm sick of it
J'en ai ras le bol	I've had enough

After leaving school

Je travaille dur	I work hard
pour que je puisse	so that I can
trouver un bon travail	find a good job
le chômage	unemployment
travailler	to work
faire un stage en entreprise	do work experience
Il travaille comme	he works as a
un boulot, un métier	job
bien payé	well-paid
à plein temps	full-time
à temps partiel	part-time
un travail temporaire	a temporary job
un travail permanent	a permanent job
il faut poser sa candidature	you have to apply

gagner un bon salaire	earn a good salary
beaucoup de chômage	high unemployment
un vendeur / une vendeuse	salesperson
un / une professeur	teacher
un chauffeur	driver
un facteur	postman *(factory of letters)*
un médecin	doctor *(medicine)*
un pharmacien	chemist
un chirurgien	surgeon *(shurgeon)*
un comptable	accountant
un avocat / une avocate	lawyer *(advocate)*
un informaticien /-ienne	IT consultant
un / une secrétaire	secretary
un serveur / une serveuse	waiter
un ingénieur	engineer
un pompier	fireman *(pumps)*
un plombier	plumber *(pb= lead)*
un gendarme	policeman
un infirmier / une infirmière	nurse *(infirmary)*
un coiffeur / -euse	hairdresser *(quiff)*
un photographe	photographer
un commerçant	shopkeeper
un ouvrier / une ouvrière	worker
un homme d'affaires	businessman
faire du bénévolat	to do voluntary work

How much can you remember?

How does the verb aller go in the present tense?

What is it followed by to make the near future tense?

What are the simple future tense endings?

Which verbs take an irregular future root?

What is that irregular root?

For your oral and writing

Favourite subjects Ma matière préférée c'est le français parce que j'ai de bonnes notes, je le trouve facile et le prof est sympa. Je n'aime pas le latin parce que je le trouve ennuyeux, le prof est nul et il nous donne trop de devoirs. Aussi, j'étudie les maths, les sciences, l'anglais, le sport, le dessin, la musique, la géo et l'histoire.

My favourite subject is French because I get good marks, I find it easy and the teacher is nice. I don't like Latin because I find it boring, the teacher is rubbish and gives us too much homework. I also do maths, science, English, sport, art, music, geography and history.

School uniform A mon école on doit porter un uniforme. Je porte un pantalon noir, une chemise blanche, des chaussures noires, des chaussettes noires, une cravate et une veste. Bien que l'uniforme soit utile pour encourager la discipline, je trouve qu'on ne peut pas montrer son individualité quand tout le monde se ressemble. J'aurais peut-être du mal au début si je devais penser à mes vêtements tous les jours, mais cela dit, j'aimerais mieux imiter le système français et m'habiller comme je veux.

At my school we have to wear a uniform. I wear black trousers, a white shirt, black shoes, black socks, a tie and a jacket. Although uniform is useful to encourage discipline, I find that you can't show your individuality when everyone looks the same. I might find it hard at first if I had to think about my clothes every day but having said that, I would rather do as the French do and wear what I like.

Homework Normalement je fais mes devoirs dans la cuisine, mais hier soir j'ai dû les faire dans ma chambre parce qu'on avait des invités. Je trouve les devoirs utiles pour pratiquer ce qu'on a appris, mais si j'étais prof je ne les donnerais pas chaque semaine. Parfois on devrait avoir le droit de se détendre un peu.

Normally I do my homework in the kitchen but last night I had to do it in my bedroom because we had visitors. I find homework useful to practice what we have learnt, but if I was a teacher, I wouldn't give it every week. Sometimes we should be able to relax a bit.

Clubs after school A mon collège on peut faire de la natation, jouer au foot ou au badminton et il y a des clubs d'échecs, de foot et de lecture. J'ai de la chance parce que je ne m'ennuie jamais. Moi je fais de l'aviron le samedi et je joue au tennis pour mon équipe scolaire.

At my school you can do swimming, play football or badminton and there are chess, football and reading clubs. I'm lucky because I never get bored. I do rowing on a Saturday and I play tennis for my school team.

Future education Pour le bac, j'étudierai la géographie, la philosophie et l'économie parce que ce sont mes matières préférées et j'ai de bonnes notes. En plus, les profs sont sympas donc j'espère qu'ils ne nous donneront pas trop de devoirs. Je devrai travailler dur pendant les deux ans, bien que ce soit ennuyeux, pour que je puisse continuer mes études à l'université. Je voudrais aller à l'université d'Oxford pour étudier l'économie. Après avoir fini mes études, il faudra que je trouve un emploi où je peux gagner un énorme salaire, afin de pouvoir prendre la retraite à trente-cinq ans.

For my A levels I will study geography, philosophy and economics because they are my favourite subjects and I get good grades. Also, the teachers are nice so I hope they won't give us too much homework. I will have to work hard over the two years although it's boring, so that I can continue my studies at university. I'd like to go to Oxford University to study economics. When I've finished studying I'll have to find a job where I can earn an enormous salary in order to be able to retire at 35.

Staying healthy in the future Quand je serai adulte je vais continuer à faire du sport, bien que ce soit fatigant, afin de pouvoir rester en forme et éviter les maladies comme l'obésité et le diabète. Je vais m'abonner à un centre sportif et passer tout mon temps libre à m'entraîner.

When I'm older I'm going to carry on doing sport, although it's tiring, so that I can keep fit and avoid illnesses like obesity and diabetes. I will join a fitness club and spend all my free time training.

Future job Je ne sais pas encore ce que je vais faire mais il faut que ce soit intéressant et passionnant. Avant tout je voudrais gagner tous les tournois de tennis et être champion du monde. Sinon, j'aimerais être prof pour que je puisse profiter des longues vacances ! Et je voudrais travailler avec les jeunes car c'est plus enrichissant que bosser dans un bureau.

I don't know yet what I'm going to do but it's got to be interesting and exciting. Above all I would like to win all the tennis tournaments and be world champion. Otherwise I'd like to be a teacher so I can make the most of the long holidays, and I'd like to work with young people because it's more gratifying than working in an office.

How to get a job Pour trouver un emploi, il faut d'abord poser sa candidature, en remplissant des fiches, avant d'assister à un entretien.

To find a job, you have to apply by filling in forms before attending an interview.

Unemployment Malheureusement, il y a un grand problème de chômage en Angleterre, surtout pour les jeunes qui viennent de terminer leurs études, et si on n'est pas suffisamment qualifié, on peut avoir du mal à trouver un boulot. J'ai horreur d'être au chômage à l'avenir. Les chômeurs risquent d'être atteints de la dépression et ne reçoivent que de ridicules allocations.

Unfortunately, there is a big unemployment problem in England, especially for young people who have just finished school, and if you're not sufficiently qualified you can struggle to find a job. I am terrified of being unemployed in the future. The unemployed are at risk of depression and only get very small benefits.

NOTES

Day 7

In this session you will be revising:

- The conditional tense
- How to talk about the ideal
- The technology topic

The conditional tense

"If I **had** time.................... I **would play** tennis"
 imperfect   conditional

Formation

To form the conditional, take the future stem (usually the infinitive) and add the imperfect endings:

manger	**répondre**	**finir**
je manger**ais**	je répondr**ais**	je finir**ais**
tu manger**ais**	tu répondr**ais**	tu finir**ais**
il manger**ait**	il répondr**ait**	il finir**ait**
nous manger**ions**	nous répondr**ions**	nous finir**ions**
vous manger**iez**	vous répondr**iez**	vous finir**iez**
ils manger**aient**	ils répondr**aient**	ils finir**aient**

But the same list of irregular future stems (ser, aur, ir, fer etc) applies as for the future tense.

Tu irais	You would go
Elle serait	She would be
Vous auriez	You would have
On ferait	We would do
Je saurais	I would know
Il pourrait	He would be able to (he could)
On devrait	We would have to (we should)

Si j'étais riche, j'achèterais un bateau.
If I was rich, I would buy a boat.

S'il y avait plus de pistes cyclables, je serais plus content.
If there were more cycle paths, I would be happier.

Si les profs donnaient moins de devoirs, je ferais plus de sport.
If the teachers gave us less homework, I would do more sport.

Si je pouvais changer quelque chose, je construirais une piscine.
If I could change something, I would build a swimming pool.

Practise the conditional tense

1. I would do — je ferais
2. I would have — j'aurais
3. I would be — je serais
4. I would have to — je devrais
5. I would be able to — je pourrais
6. It would be — ce serait
7. There would be a pool — il y aurait une piscine
8. It would be good weather — il ferait beau
9. I would change the uniform — je changerais l'uniforme
10. I'd live in Spain — j'habiterais en Espagne
11. I would go to London — j'irais à Londres
12. I'd like to learn the piano — j'aimerais apprendre le piano
13. I would try Chinese — j'essayerais le chinois
14. If I could, I'd go cycling — si je pouvais, je ferais du vélo
15. If I was rich I'd be happy — si j'étais riche, je serais content
16. If I had the time I'd go on foot — si j'avais le temps, j'irais à pied
17. If it was hot I'd go out — s'il faisait chaud, je sortirais

Vocabulary

mon portable	my mobile
mon ordinateur	my computer
je m'en sers pour	I use it to
je l'utilise pour	I use it to
envoyer des messages	to send messages
télécharger de la musique	to download music
accéder à l'internet	to go on the internet
rester à la page	to stay up to date
mettre à jour	to update
mon profil Facebook	my Facebook profile
rester en contact	to stay in touch
j'y suis accro	I'm addicted to it
scotché à l'écran	glued to the screen
je ne pourrais pas m'en passer	I couldn't do without it
le cyber-intimidation	cyber-bullying
les inconnus	strangers
le vol d'identité	identity theft
les sites de rencontre	chat rooms
les réseaux sociaux	social networks
rencontrer en ligne	to meet online
une tablette	tablet
un logiciel malveillant	malware
le piratage	hacking
en conduisant	while driving
en traversant la rue	while crossing the road
on peut avoir un accident	you can have an accident

Summary of tenses and how to recognise them

Present (but be aware of irregulars)

-e –es –e ons ez ent

-s –s –d ons ez ent

-is –is –it issons issez issent

Passé composé

Person, auxiliary (avoir or être) and past participle (mostly with é, u or i). Watch out for irregular past participles (bu, lu, pu, vu, voulu, fait, pris etc) and remember to agree them after être (house) verbs.

Imperfect

Take the nous form, take the *ons* off, add the endings: **-ais – ais –ait –ions –iez –aient**

Near future

Present tense of aller plus infinitive – easy!

Simple future (not so simple)

Add the endings that look like avoir **-ai -as -a -ons -ez -ont** onto the end of the infinitive OR onto the end of a special future stem:

Conditional

Future stem plus imperfect ending

How much can you remember?

Where do we get the root to make the conditional?

What are the conditional endings?

Which other tense shares these endings?

What is the English equivalent to *je serais?*

Which tense do we use in conjunction with the conditional to make an *if* sentence?

For your oral and writing

Technology La technologie est importante pour beaucoup de raisons. Je viens de recevoir un nouveau portable pour mon anniversaire et j'y suis accro. Je m'en sers pour tout - pour :
- rester en contact avec mes parents
- aider avec les devoirs
- envoyer des messages sur les réseaux sociaux
- télécharger des films et de la musique et jouer sur les applis.

Cependant il y a beaucoup de dangers. Par exemple on peut facilement devenir accro. Si on traverse la rue en regardant l'écran on peut facilement avoir un accident. De plus, il y a le risque de cyber-harcèlement / cyber-intimidation, de piratage et de vol d'identité.

Technology is important for lots of reasons. I have just received a new mobile for my birthday, and I'm addicted to it. I use it for everything, for staying in touch with my parents, for helping with homework, to send messages on social networks, for downloading films and music and playing on the apps. However there are lots of dangers. For example, one can easily become addicted. If you cross the road while looking at the screen you can easily have an accident. Moreover, there is the risk of cyber-bullying, hacking and identity theft.

Answers requiring the conditional tense

Ideal weekend Mon week-end idéal serait chez moi avec ma famille et mes amis. Je jouerais au foot dans le jardin, j'irais au cinéma pour voir un film d'action et je mangerais dans un bon restaurant. Le lendemain j'irais à la piscine pour faire de la natation et après être rentré chez moi je regarderais un film sur Netflix, en mangeant des bonbons.

My ideal weekend would be at home with my family and friends. I would play football in the garden, I'd go to the cinema to see an action film and I'd eat in a good restaurant. The next day I'd go to the pool to swim and after coming home I would watch a film on Netflix while eating sweets.

Ideal job   Je voudrais bien travailler à l'étranger pour que je puisse pratiquer mon français et mon espagnol. Après avoir étudié pendant autant d'années ce serait dommage de tout abandonner.

I would like to work abroad so I could practise my French and Spanish. After studying for so many years it would be a shame to give it all up.

Ideal house Ma maison idéale serait énorme avec deux grandes piscines et beaucoup de chambres pour que mes amis puissent m'y rendre visite. Aussi, il y aurait un spa et un gymnase pour que je puisse rester en forme et un court de tennis où je pourrais m'entraîner. Il y aurait un grand jardin avec beaucoup de fleurs et des arbres. Il faut que ce soit situé dans une ville animée comme Londres.

My ideal house would be enormous with two big swimming pools and lots of bedrooms so my friends could come and visit me. Also there would be a spa and a gym so I could keep fit and a tennis court where I could train. There would be a big garden with lots of flowers and trees. It would have to be situated in a lively town like London.

What you would change about your routine Si je pouvais changer quelque chose, je voudrais me lever plus tard et commencer l'école à midi, car je suis toujours fatigué le matin, et les scientifiques ont prouvé que les ados ont besoin de plus de sommeil le matin.

If I could change something, I would like to get up later and start school at midday as I'm always tired in the mornings, and scientists have proved that teenagers need more sleep in the morning.

Ideal school Mon collège idéal serait grand, moderne, tout près de chez moi pour que je puisse y aller à pied. Il y aurait une énorme piscine et un cinéma. Les cours commenceraient à midi et termineraient à quinze heures. Il n'y aurait pas d'uniforme et on ne serait pas obligé d'aller au cours de maths.

My ideal school would be big, modern and very near my home so I could go there on foot. There would be an enormous swimming pool and a cinema. Lessons would begin at midday and would finish at 3pm. There would be no uniform and we wouldn't have to go to maths lessons.

What you'd change at your school Si je pouvais changer quelque chose, je changerais l'uniforme car c'est ennuyeux de porter la même chose tous les jours. Je voudrais plutôt porter un jean, un T-shirt et des baskets. En plus, je changerais l'horaire scolaire et l'emploi du temps, parce que les scientifiques ont prouvé que les ados ont besoin de plus de sommeil le matin. Si je pouvais commencer et terminer plus tard, je pourrais me concentrer mieux et j'aurais de meilleures notes.

If I could change something, I would change the uniform as it's boring wearing the same thing every day. I'd rather wear jeans, a Tshirt and trainers. Also, I would change the school timetable because scientists have proved that teenagers need more sleep in the mornings. If I could start and finish later, I would be able to concentrate better and I would get better grades.

NOTES

Day 8

In this session you will be revising:

- The subjunctive mood
- The environment topic
- Social issues

The subjunctive mood

Although this isn't strictly a tense, it's a form of the verb that the French use all the time and using it in your speaking and writing can really earn you points. It is used after *que* in expressions relating to "so that" and "although", importance, negative thinking, emotion and wanting someone to do something. Remember SINEW

How to form the subjunctive

To form it, the general rule is that you take the 3rd person plural of the present tense, remove *ent* and add: -e -es -e -ions -iez -ent

Que je prenne   from *prendre*
Que tu viennes   from *venir*
Qu'elle finisse   from *finir*
Qu'il joue   from *jouer*

Irregular subjunctives include

être – je sois   avoir – j'aie
aller – j'aille   faire – je fasse
pouvoir – je puisse   savoir – je sache

Use it to express purpose with *pour que* and *bien que*

On doit protéger l'environnement (bien que ce soit difficile) <u>pour que nos enfants puissent</u> survivre.
We must protect the environment (although it may be difficult) so our children can survive.

J'achèterai une énorme maison (bien que ce soit cher) <u>pour que mes amis puissent</u> me rendre visite.
I will buy an enormous house (although it may be expensive) so that my friends can visit me.

Il faut sensibiliser les jeunes aux dangers du tabac (bien que ce soit ennuyeux) <u>pour qu'ils sachent</u> la vérité.
We must make young people aware of the dangers of tobacco (although it's boring) so that they know the truth.

Use it with expressions concerning the importance / necessity of someone else doing something

Il faut que tu <u>fasses</u> des efforts.
You've got to make an effort. (It is necessary that you make)

Il faut que le gouvernement <u>agisse</u>.
The government must act. (It is necessary that it act)

Il faut que nous <u>soyons</u> prudents.
We've got to be careful. (It is necessary that we be)

Il faut qu'il <u>prenne</u> ses comprimés.
He must take his pills. (It is necessary that he take)

BUT use il faut with an infinitive to express general importance

Il faut porter un uniforme.
We have to wear a uniform. (It is necessary to wear)

Use it after negative thinking

Je ne pense pas que ce <u>soit</u> une bonne idée.
I don't think it's a good idea.

Je doute qu'il <u>ait</u> fini.
I doubt he has finished.

Use it with emotions

Je suis heureux qu'il <u>soit</u> là.
I'm happy that he's there.

Je suis ravi que tu <u>sois</u> venu.
I am delighted that you came.

Use it to express what people want others to do

Ma mère veut que je <u>fasse</u> mes devoirs.
My mother wants me to do my homework.

Il veut que je <u>prenne</u> le bus.
He wants me to take the bus

Practise the subjunctive in some good oral / writing sentences

1. I'm going to continue doing sport, although it's tiring so that I can participate in competitions.
2. I'm going to buy a house in Spain, although it's complicated, so that I can improve my Spanish.
3. I'm going to go live in the countryside, although there's no public transport, so that I can breathe more easily.
4. My parents want me to go to university, although it's expensive, so that I can find a job.
5. I don't think it's a good idea.
6. It's important that we make an effort to avoid sugar.
7. I'm happy that my friends are there for me.

Answers

1. Je vais continuer à faire du sport, bien que ce soit fatigant, pour que je puisse participer a des concours.
2. Je vais acheter une maison en Espagne, bien que ce soit compliqué, pour que je puisse améliorer mon espagnol.
3. Je vais habiter à la campagne, bien qu'il n'y ait pas de transport en commun, pour que je puisse respirer plus facilement.
4. Mes parents veulent que j'aille à l'université, bien que ça coute cher, pour que je puisse trouver un travail.
5. Je ne pense pas que ce soit une bonne idée.
6. Il est important qu'on fasse (or que nous fassions) un effort pour éviter le sucre.
7. Je suis content que mes amis soient là pour moi.

Vocabulary

le changement climatique	climate change
la déforestation	deforestation
la pluie acide	acid rain
les tremblements de terre	earthquakes
l'énergie nucléaire	nuclear energy
les ressources naturelles	natural resources
en danger	in danger
les espaces verts	green spaces
la circulation	traffic
les embouteillages	traffic jams
les camions	lorries
les usines	factories
la sécheresse	drought
les inondations	floods (inundated)
les incendies	fires
les ordures / déchets	rubbish
la déchetterie	the tip
les poubelles	bins
le déboisement	deforestation

Top tip: Imagine having a shower, then turning the light off, going down and putting out the recycling, getting on the bus and going shopping for green products…

Je me douche	I shower
Je ferme les robinets	I turn the taps off
pour économiser de l'eau	to save water
J'éteins les lumières	I turn off the lights
Je recycle les emballages	I recycle packaging
J'utilise	I use
les transports en commun	public transport
J'achète des produits bio	I buy organic products
des produits écologiques	green products
on doit / il faut	we must
continuer à	to carry on
J'essaie de	I try to
Je fais des efforts pour	I make an effort to
protéger	to protect
éteindre	to switch off
fermer les robinets	to turn off the taps
économiser	to save
recycler	to recycle
trier	to sort out
les emballages	packaging
le verre	glass
le plastique	plastic
le carton	cardboard
utiliser	to use

acheter	to buy
éviter	to avoid
voyager	to travel
manifester contre	to protest against
l'effet de serre	greenhouse effect
le réchauffement global	global warming
le changement climatique	climate change

Social issues

la pauvreté	poverty
la faim	hunger
le terrorisme	terrorism
l'immigration	immigration
accueillir	to welcome
le racisme	racism
le chômage	unemployment
le taux	the rate
est en hausse	is going up
le manque de	the lack of
l'obésité	obesity
la malbouffe	junk food
les sans-abris	the homeless
les SDF (sans domicile fixe)	the homeless
Il faut qu'on fasse	we must do

quelque chose	something
quelque chose d'utile	something useful
pour les aider	to help them
les défavorisés	the less fortunate
le travail bénévole	voluntary work
les organisations caritatives	charities
les bénévoles	volunteers
consacrer du temps	to devote time
collecter de l'argent	to raise money
sensibiliser	to make aware

How much can you remember?
What does SINEW stand for?

What is the story to help us remember what we do for the environment?

Name 4 social problems we can talk about in French.

For your oral and writing

Environmental problems Le plus grand problème c'est la pollution. Les voitures et les usines produisent des gaz toxiques qui causent le réchauffement de la planète et l'effet de serre.

Pour protéger la planète: (change these to past or use infinitives after *on devrait – one should*)

- Je me douche pour économiser de l'eau (je me suis douché)
- J'éteins les lumières quand je quitte une pièce (j'ai éteint)
- Je recycle le verre, le plastique et le papier (j'ai recyclé)
- J'utilise les transports en commun (j'ai utilisé)
- J'achète des produits écologiques (j'ai acheté)

The biggest problem is pollution. Cars and factories produce toxic gases which cause global warming and the greenhouse effect. To protect the planet I shower to save water, I turn out the lights when I leave a room, I recycle glass, plastic and paper, I use public transport and I buy ecological products.

Climate change Le climat est en train de changer, il n'y a aucun doute. Il ne neige plus en hiver, tandis que pendant les années quatre-vingt il neigeait souvent. Le réchauffement de la terre a déjà causé l'augmentation du niveau des océans et il y a des îles qui commencent à disparaître. En plus il y a de plus en plus d'ouragans et de tempêtes. Je trouve tout ça effrayant, car il me semble que c'est en cherchant une meilleure vie que nous détruisons notre planète.

There is no doubt that climate change is happening. It doesn't snow anymore in winter, whereas in the 80s it snowed a lot. Global warming has already caused ocean levels to rise and some islands are disappearing. Also, there are more and more hurricanes and storms. I find all that frightening, as it seems to me that it is in searching for a better life that we are destroying our planet.

Climate change solution Il faut qu'on fasse des efforts pour changer nos habitudes, consommer moins, voyager moins, gaspiller moins d'énergie et utiliser l'énergie renouvelable comme l'énergie solaire et éolienne. On devrait utiliser les transports en commun, recycler plus et construire plus de pistes cyclables pour encourager les gens à abandonner leurs voitures.

We've got to make an effort to change our habits, consume less, travel less, waste less energy and use renewable energy like solar and wind power. We should be using public transport, doing more recycling and building more cycle paths to encourage people to leave their cars at home.

Consequences of not acting Si on ne protège pas la planète, il n'y aura bientôt plus de ressources naturelles, le trou dans la couche d'ozone grandira, et la race humaine disparaîtra. Il faut qu'on fasse des efforts pour éviter cet avenir. En famille on recycle tout ce qu'on peut – le verre, le plastique, le papier et le carton et on va à la déchetterie pour recycler les choses plus grandes comme les meubles dont on n'a plus besoin. C'est important de recycler pour économiser nos ressources naturelles et parce qu'il n'y aura bientôt plus de place dans les décharges pour tous nos déchets.

If we don't protect the planet, soon we will run out of natural resources, the hole in the ozone layer will get bigger and the human race will disappear. We need to make an effort to avoid this outcome. In my family we recycle everything we can – glass, plastic, paper and cardboard, and we go to the tip to recycle bigger things like furniture which we don't need anymore. It's important to recycle to conserve our natural resources and because soon there won't be any more space in landfill for all our rubbish.

What you do for the environment at school Au collège, tout le monde fait beaucoup d'efforts pour protéger l'environnement. On a des poubelles de recyclage dans toutes les salles de classe, on éteint les lumières quand on sort d'une pièce, et on encourage les élèves à prendre le bus au lieu de la voiture pour aller au collège.

At school everyone makes a big effort to protect the environment. We have recycling bins in all the classrooms, we turn off the lights when we leave a room and the pupils are encouraged to use public transport instead of the car to travel to school.

Social problems Il y a un grand problème de pauvreté et de chômage en Angleterre. Il y a beaucoup de sans-abris et c'est très triste quand on voit les gens qui dorment dans la rue. Si j'avais plus de temps libre, j'aiderais dans un abri pour les SDF. Je pense que c'est très important de faire du bénévolat. Ma cousine travaille dans un magasin de Oxfam une fois par semaine. J'aimerais faire du bénévolat aussi mais en ce moment les profs nous donnent trop de devoirs.

There is a big poverty and unemployment problem in England. There are many homeless people and it's very sad when you see them sleeping in the street. If I had more free time, I would help in a homeless shelter. I think it's important to do volunteering. My cousin works in an Oxfam shop once a week. I would like to volunteer too but at the moment the teachers give us too much homework.

Importance of news Les infos sont importantes parce qu'il faut qu'on sache ce qui se passe dans le monde pour avoir une opinion là-dessus. Si on n'est pas suffisamment informé, on peut être berné par les médias.

News is important because we need to know what's going on in the world in order to have an opinion on it. If you're not well-informed enough you can get brainwashed by the media.

What's in the news at the moment? Actuellement c'est le climat qui fait la une - il y a des inondations partout, des tremblements de terre et des ouragans et des centaines de maisons ont été détruites. En plus il y a la situation politique en Europe, que je trouve de plus en plus inquiétante.

Right now it's climate that's making the headlines – there are floods everywhere, earthquakes and hurricanes and hundreds of houses have been destroyed. Also there is the political situation in Europe which I find more and more worrying.

Do you read a paper? Je ne lis pas le journal, parce que je trouve que c'est plus vite en ligne et j'ai l'application de la BBC sur mon portable qui me prévient chaque fois qu'il y a quelque chose d'important à savoir.

I don't read the paper because I find it's faster online and I have the BBC app on my phone which notifies me every time there's something important to know.

Which is the most popular newspaper? Je pense que les journaux les plus populaires ce sont les journaux de petit format, les journaux à sensation. Ils ne contiennent rien d'intéressant, et ils ne servent qu'à faire peur aux gens en leur disant par exemple que le gouvernement est nul, que tout est un désastre. Je déteste ces journaux.

I think that the most popular newspapers are the sensationalist tabloids. They don't have anything interesting in them and all they do is frighten people by saying for example that our country is about to be invaded by Muslims, that the government is no good, that everything is a disaster. I hate those newspapers.

NOTES

Day 9

In this session you will be revising:

- Special constructions
- Negatives
- Weighing up pros and cons
- General vocabulary

Special constructions

There are a number of constructions that you should use in your speaking and writing to show off your French to the highest level. These include the following (and I have used the verb *manger* just as an example):

Après avoir mangé	after eating
Avant de manger	before eating
En train de manger	in the middle of eating
Je viens de manger	I have just eaten
J'ai dû manger	I had to eat
Je passe mon temps à manger	I spend my time eating
En mangeant	while eating
J'aurais dû manger	I should have eaten
J'aurais pû manger	I could have eaten
J'ai besoin de manger	I need to eat
J'ai envie de manger	I want to eat / feel like eating
Il y a cinq ans	5 years ago
J'y habite depuis [cinq ans]	I've been living there for []
J'ai de la chance	I'm lucky
Où on peut manger	where one can eat

Try translating this:

I'm lucky because I've lived there for 5 years and there are lots of parks where you can play tennis and cinemas where, after eating dinner, I spend my time watching films when I could have done my homework.

J'ai de la chance parce que j'y habite depuis cinq ans et il y a beaucoup de parcs où on peut jouer au tennis et des cinémas où, après avoir mangé, je passe mon temps à regarder des films quand j'aurais pu faire mes devoirs.

Negatives

You can impress examiners by using a number of negative structures in your writing and speaking.

Ne….. pas around a verb makes any verb negative.

Je ne bois pas	I don't drink
Je ne pense pas	I don't think

Put it **around the auxiliary** in the past tense

Je n'ai pas mangé	I didn't eat
Nous n'avons pas bu	we didn't drink

Put it **around the modal verb** in other structures

Elle ne doit pas aller	she doesn't have to go
Ils ne vont pas sortir	they aren't going to go out
On ne peut pas porter	we can't wear

Put it together only in front of an infinitive

Il a dit de ne pas attendre	he said not to wait
J'ai décidé de ne pas sortir	I decided not to go out

Substitute the *pas* for **jamais** to mean never

Je ne chante jamais	I never sing

Substitute the *pas* for **plus** to mean no longer

Je ne travaille plus	I no longer work

Substitute the *pas* for que to mean **only**

Je ne regarde que les infos	I only watch the news

Personne is a special case

Personne n'habite ici	nobody lives here
Il n'y a personne chez moi	nobody's in at my house
Je ne vois personne	I can't see anyone

Finally there is **aucun** which emphasises the *no* and agrees

Je n'ai aucune idée	I have no idea
Il n'y a aucune raison	there is no reason
Je ne vois aucune solution	I can't see any solution

Test yourself on these negative expressions

Je ne mange pas	I don't eat
Je ne mange jamais	I never eat
Je ne mange plus	I no longer eat
Je ne mange que	I only eat
Je ne mange rien	I don't eat anything
Je ne vois personne	I don't see anyone
Personne ne le fait	Nobody does it
Il n'y a personne	there's nobody there
Je n'ai aucune idée	I have no idea

Weighing up pros and cons

Lots of exam questions ask you what you think of one thing as opposed to another – do you prefer holidays with friends or family, do you prefer TV or cinema, town or countryside? It's good to have a stock of expressions to put across positive and negative aspects of things:

Positive descriptors

C'est plus …	it's more…
Il y a plus de …	there are more…
On peut facilement	you can easily
On ne doit pas	you don't have to
C'est gratuit	it's free

C'est bon marché	it's cheap
C'est moins cher / couteux	it's less expensive / pricey
Amusant	fun
Sympa	nice
Facile	easy
Rapide	fast
Bon pour la santé	good for your health
Tout ce dont j'ai besoin	everything I need
Indispensable	essential

Negative descriptors

C'est moins …	it's less…
Il n'y pas de …	there isn't / aren't any …
Il n'y a pas assez de …	there isn't / aren't enough …
Il y a moins de …	there are less / fewer…
Il y a trop de …	there is too much / there are too many
On doit	you have to
On ne peut pas	you can't
C'est cher	it's expensive
Payant	you have to pay for it
Ennuyeux	boring
Embêtant	annoying
Difficile	difficult
Lent	slow
Mauvais pour la santé	bad for your health

Vocabulary

General adjectives

plein(e)	full
vide	empty
sain(e)	healthy
malsain(e)	unhealthy
facile	easy
difficile	difficult
chaud(e)	hot
froid(e)	cold
moderne	modern
ancien (-ienne)	old
individuel(le)	detached
jumelé(e)	semi-detached
cher (chère)	expensive
bon marché	cheap
payant(e)	paying (not free)
gratuit(e)	free
sec (sèche)	dry
mouillé(e)	wet
léger (légère)	light
lourd(e)	heavy
lent(e)	slow
rapide	fast
génial(e)	great
pénible	awful

sale	dirty
propre	clean
nouveau (nouvelle)	new
étroit(e)	narrow
large	wide

Grave accent words

There aren't many of these in words that are commonly used, but don't lose marks unnecessarily by forgetting the ones you should know.

après	after
très	very
près de	near
mère / père	mother, father
frère	brother
derrière	last
derrière	behind
à (eg à gauche / à Londres)	at / to (on the left)
où	where
là	there
Je me lève	I get up
J'espère	I hope
J'achète	I buy
Je préfère (sad eyebrow accents)	I prefer
problème	problem
déjà	already
élève	pupil
collège	school

bibliothèque	library
matière	subject
complètement	completely
mystère	mystery

Here's a story to help you remember the words :

Where do I live? I live **there**, in a **very** big house **near** London **behind** the **library**, with my **mother**, **father**, **brother**, **grandmother** and **grandfather**. I hope that when I **get up, I buy** something - but the **problem** is that I have to go to **school** and be a **pupil already** studying a **subject** and I **prefer** it to be **completely** a **mystery**.

Very french things

Some places and activities are peculiar to the French.

un Parisien	person from Paris
le TGV	train à grande vitesse (fast train)
le SNCF	French railway company
le VTT	mountain biking
les randonnées	hikes
la chasse	hunting
la boulangerie	baker's shop
la pâtisserie	cake shop
quinze jours	a fortnight
le lycée	sixth form college
un lycéen	a sixth former
un département	similar to a "county" of France
les escargots	snails
en seconde	in year 12

en terminale	in year 13
redoubler	to repeat a year at school
le brevet	GCSE equivalent
un stage en entreprise	a work placement
préparer le bac	to do A levels
une commune	a village
la mairie	the town hall
faire la bise	to kiss on both cheeks
La Marseillaise	the national anthem
le tricolore	the French flag

How much can you remember?

Name ten French words with grave accents.

Name six positive and six negative descriptors.

What is the rule about the position of *ne* and *pas*?

For your oral and writing

Advantages of living in a town L'avantage d'habiter en ville c'est qu'il y a tout ce dont j'ai besoin et plein de choses à faire. En plus je peux facilement retrouver mes amis en utilisant les transports en commun. Je trouve les bus indispensables. Je m'en sers tous les jours et je ne pourrais pas m'en passer.

The advantage of living in town is that there is everything I need and lots of things to do. Also, I can easily meet up with my friends using public transport. I find the buses essential. I use them every day and couldn't manage without them.

Disadvantages of living in a town Ce que je n'aime pas tellement c'est la pollution de l'air causée par les gaz d'échappement. La pollution provoque le réchauffement de la terre et l'effet de serre mais il me semble que les gens sont trop égoïstes pour abandonner le confort de leurs voitures et prendre le bus. En plus, il n'y a pas assez de pistes cyclables. S'il y en avait plus, j'irais partout à vélo.

What I don't like so much is the air pollution caused by car emissions. Pollution causes global warming and the greenhouse effect, but it seems that people are too selfish to abandon the comfort of their cars and take the bus. Also, there aren't enough cycle paths. If there were more, I'd go everywhere by bike.

Advantages of the countryside A la campagne c'est moins pollué qu'en ville et il y a plus d'espaces verts où on peut se promener et respirer l'air frais. Les prix immobiliers sont plus bas car le terrain coûte moins cher. Il y a beaucoup moins de circulation, donc on peut faire du vélo sans avoir peur d'être écrasé par un bus.

In the countryside it's less polluted than in the town and there are more green spaces where you can walk and breathe fresh air. The house prices are lower as land is cheaper. There is a lot less traffic so you can cycle without worrying about being run over by a bus.

Disadvantages of the countryside A la campagne, bien que ce soit plus tranquille et plus calme, il n'y a rien à faire et on doit aller partout en voiture car il n'y a pas de transports en commun. Je ne voudrais jamais y habiter car je me sentirais trop isolé.

In the countryside, although it's quieter and calmer, there isn't anything to do and you have to go everywhere by car as there is no public transport. I would never want to live there as I'd feel too isolated.

Holidays with parents v holidays with friends Si on part en vacances avec les parents, c'est facile et c'est gratuit. Ils paient tout et on ne doit penser à rien. Cependant, c'est eux qui décident ce qui est permis, et on n'a pas beaucoup de choix. Ils me trainent aux musées les plus ennuyeux du monde et j'en ai marre. Avec les amis, on peut s'amuser beaucoup plus, on peut sortir quand on veut, rentrer quand on veut et manger ce qu'on veut. J'ai hâte de partir avec mes copains dès que j'aurai l'occasion.

If you go on holiday with parents, it's easy and free. They pay for everything and you don't need to think about anything. However, they are the ones that decide what is allowed and you don't get much choice. They drag me round the most boring museums in the world and I'm sick of it. With friends you can have much more fun, you can go out when you like, come back when you like and eat what you like. I can't wait to go away with my friends as soon as I get the chance.

Cinema or TV? Je préfère le cinéma parce que c'est plus passionnant que rester dans le salon. J'aime les films d'action parce qu'il y a de bons effets spéciaux. Cependant, les billets coutent les yeux de la tête et je n'ai pas les moyens d'y aller plus qu'une fois par mois.

I prefer the cinema because it's more exciting that staying in the living room. I like action films because there are good special effects. However, the tickets cost the earth and I can't afford to go more than once a month.

NOTES

Day 10

In this session you will be revising:

- How to do a good essay using the writing mnemonic – an alphabetical list L-V of things to remember when writing an essay
- How to approach the listening exam
- Synonyms and homonyms
- Top ten mistakes – don't make them!

The writing mnemonic…

Leave a line so you can add things later to increase word count.

Modals

The verbs to have to, to be able to, to want to are all modal verbs and you need to show the examiner that you can use them in all tenses

J'ai dû rentrer chez moi	I had to go home
On devrait protéger l'environnement	We should protect
On peut faire du sport	One can do/play sport
Je veux être avocat	I want to be a lawyer

Negatives

Je n'ai pas d'animaux	I don't have any pets
Je ne fumerais jamais	I would never smoke
Il n'y a plus d'argent	There's no more money

Opinions

A mon avis	In my opinion
Je crois / pense que	I believe
Il me semble que	It seems to me that

Pronouns

Les profs nous donnent	The teachers give us
Je me lève	I get up
Je le trouve facile	I find it easy

Quel

Quel désastre!	What a disaster!
Quelle chance!	What luck!

Reasons

Parce que, car, puisque	because

Superlatives (and comparatives)

Le meilleur collège de Londres	The best school in London
Il est plus sportif que moi	He is more sporty than me

Time phrases

Avant de + infinitive	before (doing something)
Après avoir + past participle	After (doing something)
En arrivant	On arriving
Je viens de	I have just
Il est sur le point de	He is about to
Tous les jours	Every day

Umbrella (weather!)

Il a fait chaud / beau	It was hot
Il pleut / il neige	It is raining / snowing
Il pleuvait / il neigeait	It was raining / snowing
Il a plu / il a neigé	It rained / snowed

Verbs

Use all the tenses you can possibly cram in:

Present   eg. Je fais beaucoup de sport

Perfect   eg. Il a fait beau

Imperfect   eg. Quand j'etais jeune

Near Future   eg. Je vais aller au cinéma

Future simple   eg. Nous irons au théâtre

Conditional   eg. J'acheterais une piscine

Present subjunctive   eg. Pour que je puisse nager

Listening tips

Good exam technique

Don't panic! Everyone will find this paper the hardest part of the exam. Here are a few tips to help you keep calm:

- Trust your memory. When you listen to someone tell you what they did at the weekend, you can remember it afterwards without taking notes. Try and get used to doing the same here. If you are writing and listening at the same time, you are likely to miss something.

- Take every chance you get to read the question in advance so you know the exact information to listen out for. You are not expected to understand every word and there will be plenty of language that is irrelevant to the question you need to answer.

- Listen to the end of each passage. If you rush into answering before the speaker has finished, you may miss the crucial twist, such as she likes history, *but she really loves* geography. Pay special attention to negatives, including words like "peu de" which means *few*, rather than *a few*, so the emphasis is on the fact that there are not very many.

- Listen out for tenses. Has she got a dog now or did she have one when she was younger? Is she studying law or is she planning to in the future?

- Use your knowledge of France and French-speaking countries. Past exams have included references to *une malienne* which you will be expected to know is a female resident of Mali. Look at the list of "very French things" at the back of this book. Abbreviations such as TGV and SDF should be familiar to you.

- As well as the actual words being spoken, the tone of someone's voice may be helpful in showing their mood. The intonation of someone's voice may tell you if they are making a statement or asking a question.

Synonyms

There is more than one way of expressing most things. Just take a look at the number of ways you can express *liking* for a start…

Liking

j'aime	I like
j'adore	I love
ça me plaît	it pleases me
ça me fait plaisir	it gives me pleasure
c'est bon	it's good / tasty
je l'aime	I like it
ça fait du bien	it feels good
ça m'a plu	I liked it / it pleased me
agréable	pleasant
intéressant	interesting
passionnant	exciting
ça me passionne	it excites me
ça m'intéresse	it interests me
c'est mon truc	it's my thing
j'y suis accro	I am addicted to it

Agreement

d'accord	okay, I agree
tu as raison	you are right
je partage ton opinion	I share your opinion
je pense la même chose	I think the same thing

Disagreement

tu as tort	you are wrong
tu n'as pas raison	you are not right
tu dis des bêtises	you are talking rubbish
je ne partage pas ton avis	I don't share your opinion
je pense autrement	I think differently

Disliking

je déteste	I hate
j'ai horreur de	I hate
j'en ai marre	I'm sick of it
ça m'embête	it annoys me
c'est embêtant	it's annoying
ça m'énerve	it annoys me
c'est énervant	it's annoying
ce n'est pas mon truc	it's not my thing
nul	rubbish

Students

les élèves	pupils
les lycéens	sixthformers
les étudiants	students

A method, manner or way of doing something

une méthode	method
une façon	fashion or means
un moyen	a means

une manière — a manner

To talk

parler de — talk about
discuter de — discuss
bavarder — to chat
tchatter — to chat online
papoter — to chat (familiar)

Jobs

le travail — work
un poste — a post / job
un emploi — a job
un boulot — a job
un métier — a job
une carrière — a career
les ouvriers — workers
les salariés — workers
les syndicats — trade unions
la classe ouvrière — the working classes
le chômage — unemployment
faire la grève — to strike
une société — a company or society
une entreprise — a company / enterprise
renvoyer — to sack
licencier — to sack
manifester — to protest

Prices

bon marché	cheap
cher	expensive
pas cher	not expensive
couteux	costly
moins cher	less expensive
moins couteux	less costly
plus cher	more expensive
plus couteux	more costly
prix bas	low prices
prix élévés	high prices
gratuit	free
payant	not free

Not allowed

on ne peut pas	one cannot
c'est interdit	it is forbidden
ce n'est pas permis	it's not permitted
on ne permet pas	one does not allow
il ne faut pas	one must not
on n'a pas le droit	we can't / we don't have the right

Essential

il faut	it is necessary
on doit	one must
obligatoire	obligatory / compulsory
primordial	essential

essentiel	essential
inéluctable	inevitable
obligé de	obliged to
il n'y a pas de choix	there is no choice

Food

la nourriture	food
les aliments	food items
l'alimentation	food
la cuisine	cuisine / food
un repas	a meal
un plat	a dish

how often ?

toujours	always
sans exception	without exception
dans tous les cas	in every case
sans arrêter	without stopping
souvent	often
de temps en temps	sometimes
parfois	sometimes
sauf le jeudi	except on Thursdays
presque toujours	nearly always

To keep healthy

rester en forme	to stay healthy
garder la forme	to keep fit

avoir une bonne santé	to be in good health
suivre un régime	to be on a diet
manger sain(ement)	to eat healthily
éviter	to avoid

To move

bouger	to move (generally)
se déplacer	to move around (by any means)
circuler	to move around (transport)
déménager	to move house

Funny

drôle	funny
marrant	funny
amusant	fun
rigolo	funny (from rigoler – to giggle)
il me fait rire	it makes me laugh
sourire	to smile

Teaching

le / la prof	teacher
une maîtresse	teacher (mistress)
un instituteur	teacher (man)
une institutrice	teacher (woman)
l'enseignant(e)	teacher (general)
enseigner	to teach
apprendre	to learn or teach

Homonyms

Some words have the same sound but different meanings. You will need to work out the meaning from the context. Here are some examples of typical homonyms (or words that can sound very similar) that can really confuse students in listening exams.

vent (wind)	vend (sells)	
voit (sees)	voix (voice)	
verre (glass)	vert (green)	vers (towards)
pois (peas)	poids (weight)	
dos (back)	d'eau (of water)	
dans (in)	dent (tooth)	
moi (me)	mois (month)	
toi (you)	toit (roof)	
cette (this)	sept (seven)	
tente (tent)	tante (aunt)	
pris (taken)	prix (prize or price)	
ça (it)	sa (his or her)	
plus (more)	plu (pleased)	plu (rained)
plus tôt (earlier)	plutôt (rather)	
bois (wood)	bois, boit (drink)	
doigt (finger)	dois, doit (must)	
lit (bed)	lis, lit (read)	
marché (market)	marcher (to walk)	
mais (but)	mes (my)	
thé (tea)	tes (your)	
cru (raw)	cru (believed)	
mal (badly)	mâle (male)	
été (summer)	été (been)	

Listen out for added consonants

Sometimes you will have trouble identifying a word because it has an extra consonant on the front. This happens when a clash of vowels has required the previous word (je, de, le, me, que etc) to replace its last vowel with an apostrophe. If you saw it written, it wouldn't cause a problem. But on listening you can easily miss it. The shorter the word the more confusing it is. For example:

L'Inde est belle – India is beautiful

Une pièce *d'or* – a gold coin

Près *d'eux* – near them

J'ai besoin *d'air* – I need air

Je n'ai pas *d'eau* – I don't have any water

Je n'ai *qu'un* frère – I only have one brother

Ça *m'aide* à me relaxer – It helps me relax

How much can you remember?

What is the writing mnemonic?

Give examples of all the things you must include.

The top ten mistakes – don't make them!

1. **Beaucoup DE** – never des, no, not even if the thing that follows is plural, because it usually will be plural if there are lots of them!
2. We don't play sport – we do it – **je fais du sport**, no mention of jouer unless you are referring to a specific sport involving a ball
3. **The food I ate today is du, de la or des** – NEVER just de
4. **No e acutes are in the future** – try and say that as if it rhymes, and don't forget the future tense is aller + INFINITIVE
5. **Nous sommes allés has an s on the end** – sing or chant this until it is completely entrenched in your brain that past participles with être agree with the person doing it!
6. **Si je pouvais** (if I could) is essential to your speaking and writing as it leads into the conditional. You can always finish the sentence with *je voudrais avoir…*
7. **No articles with jobs** – remember it's *je veux être prof*, not *un* prof.
8. Don't mix up 'I prefer' with 'favourite'. The way to remember it is that **je préfère** is almost the same as I prefer, in that the words for prefer sound very similar in French and English. The word préféré (favourite) has three syllables and three acute accents.
9. It's **à with towns and en with countries and engine transport** – and don't mention Portugal or anywhere outside Europe to stay safe with this rule.
10. **Agree your adjectives.** I know you know how to do this so DO IT – it's such an easy way to lose marks. Ma maison est **grande**. (but after *c'est*, adjectives are always masculine!)

Other publications also available on Amazon:

How to Ace your French oral

How to Ace your Spanish oral

How to Ace your German oral

French vocabulary for GCSE

Spanish vocabulary for GCSE

The French GCSE handbook

The Spanish GCSE handbook

Advanced French Conversation

Advanced French Vocabulary

The A level French handbook

The Common Entrance French Handbook

Brush up your French – a revision guide for grown-ups

Ten Magic tricks with French

Spanish in a week

If you have any comments or questions on any of the content of this book, please do get in touch via my website

www.lucymartintuition.co.uk

Find me on Facebook and like my page to be first in the running for news and offers and free books. And for some extra tips on how to impress examiners with your oral and writing, subscribe to my Lucy Martin Tuition YouTube channel.

Printed in Great Britain
by Amazon